RETHINKING FREEDOM

RETHINKING FREEDOM

WHY FREEDOM HAS LOST ITS MEANING AND WHAT CAN BE DONE TO SAVE IT

C. FRED ALFORD

RETHINKING FREEDOM
© C. Fred Alford, 2005.

First published in 2005 by
PALGRAVE MACMILLAN™
175 Fifth Avenue, New York, N.Y. 10010 and
Houndmills, Basingstoke, Hampshire, England RG21 6XS
Companies and representatives throughout the world.

PALGRAVE MACMILLAN is the global academic imprint of the Palgrave Macmillan division of St. Martin's Press, LLC and of Palgrave Macmillan Ltd. Macmillan® is a registered trademark in the United States, United Kingdom and other countries. Palgrave is a registered trademark in the European Union and other countries.

ISBN 1–4039–6834–9
ISBN 1–4039–6872–1 (pbk.)

Library of Congress Cataloging-in-Publication Data

Alford, C. Fred.
    Rethinking freedom : why freedom lost its meaning and
what can be done to save it / C.
    Fred Alford.
        p. cm.
    Includes bibliographical references and index.
    ISBN 1–4039–6834–9—ISBN 1–4039–6872–1 (pbk.)
        1. Liberty. 2. Individuality. I. Title.

HM1266.A44 2005
323.44—dc22   2004057317

A catalogue record for this book is available from the British Library.

Design by Newgen Imaging Systems (P) Ltd., Chennai, India.

First edition: May 2005

10 9 8 7 6 5 4 3 2 1

Printed in the United States of America.

Transferred to digital printing in 2007.

To all those who talked with me about freedom

CONTENTS

Preface   ix

Chapter 1   Freedom or Power?   1

Chapter 2   Borderlines of Freedom   27

Chapter 3   Bad Faith?   55

Chapter 4   Mastery and Respite   67

Chapter 5   Freedom Is Seeing Reality Clearly   89

Chapter 6   Transgression with Others   103

Chapter 7   Aristocrats of Freedom   123

Research Appendix   141
Notes   145
References   151
Index   159

PREFACE

Almost every day the term "freedom" loses a little more of its meaning, becoming an all purpose word for everything that is good about our way of life. I think that is why I wrote this book. Or rather, it is why I went through the process of writing this book, which involved going around asking people what they thought freedom meant, comparing their answers to the answers of some of the great philosophers of freedom. Though it took me several years, I learned a lot in the process, and I think I now understand not only what the term "freedom" means but why it is so hard to get a grip on the term. Not only that, but I think I better understand the strange affinity of freedom for constraint: why so many people are willing to cover their chains with garlands of flowers, so as to call them signs of their freedom. About freedom there are daily a dozen permutations, and seldom anything new under the sun.

I think it is my friend and colleague Roger Lewin who came up with the term "freedom with," but it could have been me in discussion with him. That's the way it works with "freedom with."

From my wife Elly, I've learned about the freedom that comes from fully investing oneself in an artistic performance.

Sean Eudaily taught me about the freedom of jazz, the freedom of "in the groove."

Victor Wolfenstein taught me what Donovan had to say about freedom in his lovely song "Colours."

Lynne Layton made a number of helpful comments. I remember particularly her remark that Alasdair MacIntyre should not get all the credit for recognizing human dependence; this has been a leading theme of many feminists for several decades now.

Sam Brown directed me to "Eye Promise," but would not want to be associated with its project in any way.

Jeffrey Stepnisky told me about the General Social Survey's freedom module, and helped me gain access to the data.

CHAPTER 1
FREEDOM OR POWER?

Over the last several years, I've been talking with people about freedom. It seems like an important topic. The United States claims to be fighting for freedom all over the world. "Freedom is the president's favorite foreign policy term these days," says *The Washington Post* (June 23, 2002, B1). "Freedom is an all-purpose word he employs to define a high purpose, defend action on the ground or parry awkward questions." "Freedom itself is under attack," President George W. Bush declared in the terrible days after September 11. If the people I talked with care relatively little for freedom, and hardly at all for the political freedom about which the president of the United States is so passionate, then there is much to wonder and worry about.

Most people I spoke with informally define freedom as the possession of money and power, or they devalued freedom compared to money and power. The term "informally define" means that this is how they responded to my first question, "What's freedom?" This question was designed to elicit an informant's working definition of freedom without appearing to call for a formal definition. To be sure, money and power are not most people's last words on the subject, just the first; in one way or another, most of them who answered in this fashion said they regretted having to do so. But they did.

"Maybe money can't buy happiness, but money buys freedom. Freedom means having enough money to do what I want," said one young woman, who was echoed by many others. It was the leading theme.

"You've got to have the resources if you want to be free," said another. What resources, I asked? Money?

"No, not just money, but education, a decent job. Freedom takes power. No one is going to give it to you."

Most talked in these terms. Freedom is not about being left alone by others; nor is freedom about such effete rights as free speech. Many disparaged the concept. Partly because they took it for granted, but also because it doesn't matter if you can say what you want if you can't do what you want.

"Of course I can say anything I want," said John, one of my informants. "I have the freedom to say what I want, and you have the freedom to ignore me. So does everyone else. So what's the point? I don't want freedom to say what I want. I want freedom to do what I want."

Doesn't freedom of speech mean anything, I asked?

"Not really. It's just a symbol."

It is in this context that the comment by Anita, another of my informants, should be understood. "I've got all the freedom I need," she said. "I don't need any more freedom. What I need is some control over my own life."

What do you mean "all the freedom you need," I asked in genuine puzzlement.

"I mean that I can say what I want and nobody is going to put me in jail. But what I really need is a job that pays enough so I can work part-time and still go to school. Now that would be real freedom."

It is hard for me to convey the tone of dismissal, often bordering on contempt, with which many people spoke about what, for now, I will call formal freedom, the freedoms enshrined in the Bill of Rights for example. Nor is it a matter of a relatively privileged group of Americans (especially when compared to their beleaguered counterparts all over the world) simply assuming formal freedom as their birthright. Most did, but it would be more accurate to say that for most people I spoke with, formal freedom has been rendered meaningless by overuse and abuse of the term.

One might conclude from all this that teachers and other cultural workers should define and use the terms associated with formal freedom more precisely, so that freedom itself regains something of its original aura. My research suggests that the problem is more complex, rooted in a psychological and material reality that will not readily surrender to sound intellectual hygiene. In any case, mine is not a philosophical study of the true meaning of a term that is at risk of losing all meaning. Mine is a social, political, and psychological account of why freedom seems to have lost its meaning, and what might be done to restore it. The answer (to jump ahead to the last two chapters) has more to do with politics than philosophy.

One reason freedom has lost its meaning is because the term has become a cudgel with which to pummel political opponents. On the Diane Rheem National Public Radio talk show (February 15, 2001), a lobbyist for the assisted living industry said that what seniors want most is "freedom of choice." They hate to have their "freedom taken away," but long to have "all their options open," so that they can remain "independent and free." Sure seniors want this. We all do. But, seniors also want to be taken care of, not just to have someone there if they fall or become sick; they want to have their needs anticipated, to be comforted, to live in a predictable and secure environment, and so forth. I interviewed several seniors about freedom, and this—no surprise—is what they said. "I'm not free if I have to worry about falling or getting sick, and lying on the bathroom floor for hours. What kind of freedom is that?" is how one senior put it. Something about freedom blinds us to the otherwise obvious fact that it is the balance between autonomy and care that constitutes the experience of freedom. Characterizing this blinding "something" is the topic of my manuscript.

To be sure, the lobbyist was using the term "freedom" as former House Majority Leader Richard Armey recommends. "No matter what cause you advocate, you must sell it in the language of freedom" (Foner, 1998, 324–325). In other words, the lobbyist was using the term "freedom" in a political battle against laws regulating the quality of care in assisted living facilities. But there is something about the term, the concept, and even the experience of freedom that lends itself to this misuse. This stems, I believe, from the fact that the experience of freedom depends upon our not being constantly reminded of how dependent we are on others in virtually every aspect of our lives. Trouble is, not being reminded of this fact makes it easier to deny how much we depend on others for our freedom, indeed for our lives. In one way or another, this is the theme of my manuscript.

In *Moral Freedom*, Alan Wolfe (2001, 100, 226) writes, "the twenty-first century will be the century of moral freedom." With the term "moral freedom," he means the liberty of the individual to determine for him or herself what is right and good, not just to listen to God, but to talk back, as Wolfe puts it. Toward moral freedom, Wolfe (2001, 231) takes up an attitude like that of Alexis de Tocqueville toward democracy in *Democracy in America*, written in the 1830s to explain how democracy might be made safe for the rest of the world, especially France. Like Tocqueville on democracy, Wolfe holds that moral freedom may not be a good thing, but it's the coming thing, so we had better get used to it.

Perhaps, but it turns out that we shall have to live with more than moral freedom. We shall have to live with its counterpart, moral fear. Wolfe does not appreciate this point. Neither did I until I had completed my research and begun to think about the implications. If one value is as good as another, or at least there is no one in authority to say otherwise, not even God, then, not just moral freedom but moral fear is the outcome.

The reason, people tell me (though of course I must interpret their answers in order to reach this conclusion), is that when all values are equal, the power to get what one wants becomes the only standard. Moral freedom turns into the devaluation of freedom in the name of power, as power is the only value one can count on, the universal medium of moral exchange in a world in which all values are equal. In other words, freedom becomes a luxury. What is desired above all else is the power to protect oneself against the incursions of others. Insulation becomes freedom. Anyone familiar with Thomas Hobbes's account of the state of nature in *Leviathan*, where life is nasty, brutish, and short, will recognize the reasoning. It is surprising, however, that one finds similar reasoning among civilized citizens of a civilized society.

Moral freedom, as Wolfe calls it, leads directly to a moral fear that renders freedom largely irrelevant to people's lives. This is the unhappy conclusion to which my data have driven me. My data *are* the people I talked with. Occasionally I refer to them as informants, a term popular in the anthropological literature. The term seems appropriate. Often I felt as though I was studying a strange new tribe—American young people—comparing and contrasting their views of freedom with that of a more familiar tribe (at least to me)—middle-aged and older Americans.[1]

How strange was this tribe? The question may be read in several ways, one suggesting that the people I spoke with were atypical. True enough: my informants were younger than average, and more diverse than average. They were, in other words, no random sample of the population. Nevertheless, there was not much difference between what the people I spoke with said about freedom on a forced-choice questionnaire and what a large group of randomly selected subjects said about freedom on the General Social Survey (GSS), "generally considered the premier social science instrument for monitoring social life and trends in the United States," according to its own modest self-description. The real difference is between answering questions on a survey, many of which seem to have an ideologically correct answer, and talking about freedom in an unstructured interview. (See the Research Appendix for details of this comparison, in which I asked about 50 people—including a number who went on to talk with me about freedom, and all of whom fit the profile of the average younger informant—to answer the same questions as those on the GSS "freedom module.")

Though I spoke with people of all ages, I ended up talking with about twice as many younger informants (18–30 years) as older ones (31–74 years). One reason I focus on young people is that it was they who said the most fascinating and disturbing things about freedom. The other reason is that young people are the future. Though aspects of their views of freedom will surely mellow as they grow older, I argue (but cannot prove) that the difference between younger and older is not just a consequence of maturation. The difference has to do with the world that young people have grown up in.

Many of the young people interviewed attend, or attended, the state university where I teach. Most of them are putting or put themselves through school, and the reader should not imagine that they are students of a couple of generations ago. A number are married; quite a few have children. None are poor, but they are not well-off, and few come from wealthy families. This influences what they think about freedom. Several spoke of making decisions that revealed real economic pressure, such as being unable to have a car repaired and so taking the bus.

When I refer to "young people," I mean the young people I spoke with. While mine is a diverse sample, it is not random, and so generalizations must be made with caution. When I refer to "people," I mean all the people I spoke with, older as well as younger. Again, generalizations must be made with caution, but there is no reason to think this was an especially odd lot, and good reason to think it was not: above all the similarity between the answers of those I interviewed on the GSS and the answers of a large randomly chosen sample on the GSS.

Race is a complicated category these days. The men and women I spoke with identified themselves with half a dozen "racial" groups: white, black, Indians, Hispanics, Asians, and mixed. Cosmopolitan, with family connections all over the world, this is probably the most unusual quality of this diverse but nonrandom sample. About 70 percent were self-identified white. All but two are American citizens. Christian, Jew, Muslim, Hindu, Buddhist, and Confucian: this list does not exhaust the religious diversity of the people I talked with. Though race and ethnicity seemed to influence people's responses, the sample was not large enough to draw any conclusions. Remarkable is how similar diverse people sounded, not how different. (The Research Appendix contains more demographic details.)

The image that comes to mind is Tocqueville's fable of the forest, his account of how Americans from different walks of life seem to end up thinking and believing the same thing, even as they live in isolation from one another, at least compared to the feudal order with which Tocqueville was familiar in France. Tocqueville called this isolation "individualism." The term was not a compliment. In my version of Tocqueville's fable, the denizens of the forest are each of a different race and religion, but they all end up at the same spot, or want to.

> Variety is disappearing from within the human species. They ... become more alike even though they have not imitated each other. They are like travelers dispersed in a great forest in which all the paths end at the same point. If all perceive the central point at once and direct their steps in this direction, they are insensibly brought nearer to one another without seeking each other, without perceiving and without knowing each other, and they will finally be surprised to see themselves gathered in the same place. (Tocqueville, 2000, 588)

This place is the possession of enough money and power to protect oneself from the will of others.

Among academics with whom I have shared my results, this conclusion seems to be the most surprising: that diverse people see freedom in the same way. Aren't race, sex, and ethnicity the leading categories of existence, the experience that structures everything we hold dear? Perhaps, but not as far as freedom is concerned. In half a dozen different accents, American freedom sounds much the same. I do not know if this implies that academics should rethink the centrality of race, sex, and ethnicity. Freedom is only one dimension of experience, albeit an important one. In any case, the single most important demographic variable turns out to be age, a category not quite so popular with (aging?) academics. The second most important variable seems to be income, but there were not enough wealthy young people to draw any firm conclusions.

Most of the interviews were conducted before the terrorist attacks of September 11, 2001, but over a third were conducted afterward. That terrible event didn't seem to make much difference in how people talked about freedom. Though I didn't ask people about the terrorist attacks, there was plenty of opportunity for them to bring up the topic had they wanted to; few did. Probably because my questions were designed to evoke more personal experiences of freedom. Nothing is more important than an individual's everyday life in influencing his or her views about freedom. Even in our anxious age, everyday life for most people is dominated by such mundane concerns as making a living. This turns out to be important in understanding how people experience freedom—not as a political ideal, but as a presence or absence in their daily lives.

Perusing dozens of Internet websites devoted to freedom, I reached the same conclusion as Eric Foner (1998, 330–332) in *The Story of American Freedom*. The vast majority of sites are concerned with what can only be called paranoid freedom: the government is coming to take away your guns, your rights, your property. We enlightened few must get together to stop them. Some of these sites espoused views I agree with, such as the danger to civil liberties posed by antiterrorist legislation and the like, but that does not make these sites any less paranoid in the casual sense in which I use the term here, the world divided into those who would attack freedom and those proud few who would protect it.

All in all, the paranoid freedom into which the experience of freedom can degenerate, including the freedom to give up one's self to the latest cult, is not something that most Americans need worry about in themselves or their neighbors. About this my research is reassuring. Not a single person I spoke with even hinted at the satisfaction of giving oneself up to the cult, group, or leader. This statement requires qualification. Two anarchists I interviewed found satisfaction in losing themselves in a lawless group for a little while. But, the very nature of anarchism sets limits on that experience, and it was my impression that both informants were relieved that it did.

The freedom to give oneself over to a cult or to a charismatic leader is not something we need to worry about very much these days, at least among the mainstream population. That concern belongs to an earlier era, still horrified by Hitler and Stalin (Bay, 1970; Fromm, 1969). Today (and I am talking here only about the Western democracies), we should be more concerned with the rise of anomie and isolation associated with the belief that only individual mastery, generally equated with money, can protect the self against the intrusions of others. The danger today is that freedom will come to be equated with, or rather reduced to, power. Not even Hobbes held to such a harshly individualistic and competitive view of freedom. Or rather, he held that such a harshly individualistic and competitive view belongs to life in the state of nature. Why young people, especially, see civilized society in the terms, if not the extremes, of Hobbes's state of nature is a puzzle worth solving. Whether young people's vision is itself paranoid is also worth considering.

What Freedom?

No idea is so generally recognized as indefinite, ambiguous, and open to the greatest misconceptions . . . as the idea of Freedom: none in the common currency with so little appreciation of its meaning.

(Hegel, 1971, 239)

On occasion Hegel is truly wise, and this is one of those occasions. The question is what to do about it. I have chosen to focus on the experiences of freedom and on the constraints faced by the men and women I spoke with, letting their narrative frame my own, which runs from an analysis of what people said in this first chapter, to a diagnosis of an illness of the culture in the second.

I name this illness after a psychoanalytic category—borderline personality disorder. I do so not in order to diagnose informants, but to characterize the world they live in, much as Christopher Lasch (1979) used a psychoanalytic term, narcissism, to characterize the North American culture of the 1970s. If the 1970s was the culture of narcissism, then the 1980s and beyond might best be characterized as a culture on the borderline.

Chapters 3 through 5 weave together what people say about freedom with the sayings of several famous philosophers of freedom. Overall, this manuscript is a long, surprised reaction to what the people I talked with did and didn't say about freedom.

Jean-Paul Sartre was a French philosopher who said that I am absolutely free. No matter what happens to me, I always have a choice about how to interpret my experience, and so give it the meaning I choose. One man sent to prison will experience himself as having lost his freedom. Another may experience himself as having found his freedom there, perhaps because it is in prison that he first learned to cultivate his mind. This, at least, is what Malcolm X said. For Sartre, the problem is not that people need to be liberated; the problem is that most people fail to recognize the freedom they already have, the freedom to imagine any situation as otherwise. Sartre called this failure "bad faith." Many of the people I talked with seem to suffer from bad faith, though Sartre could learn a thing or two from them as well.

Herbert Marcuse, a philosopher who fled Germany for the United States during the Nazi era, became famous during the 1960s for his radicalism. I bought his most famous book, *One-Dimensional Man* (1964), at an airport bookshop on my way back to college in 1968. Freedom, argues Marcuse, is not about mastering my world. Freedom means abandoning myself to the claims of Orpheus and Narcissus, the charms of silence, sleep, night, and a passivity that comes close to death. One of the most fascinating aspects of listening to young people muse about freedom is the frequency with which Marcuse's themes come up, as though the desires Marcuse writes of live an underground existence in the lives of many young people. Chapter 4 is devoted to the clandestine connection between Marcuse and the younger informants.

If Sartre and Marcuse are well known, Iris Murdoch is not, at least in the United States. Murdoch, British philosopher and novelist, holds that freedom is seeing reality clearly, liberated from the claims of narcissism and convention. Why this is freedom, and not something else, such as knowledge or a taste for reality, is of course the key question. What would help people see more clearly is the chief concern of chapter 5.

Chapters 6 and 7 consider how people's experiences of freedom might be rendered political without spoiling these experiences, or turning them into someone else's experience, such as that of the political theorist. As a political theorist, I know that freedom has a political dimension, but I am not convinced that it is the most important dimension. Certainly most of the people I spoke with do not think it is. Freedom is, in the end, an individual achievement, even as we frequently experience freedom most fully in the company of others. Several famous political theorists are consulted, such as Sheldon Wolin and Hannah Arendt, but the focus remains on the way of thinking about freedom that would be most helpful to young people.

Allowing people's experience of freedom to set the boundaries of the discussion in every chapter is already a contentious act, for one might argue that freedom is not so much an experience as a concept, a part of the Great Tradition.[2] Focusing on people's experience of freedom at the expense of this tradition is to start off on the wrong foot, or so it might be argued. For those already convinced that average people can tell us nothing important about freedom, nothing I say will change their minds. The best I can do is characterize the foot I am starting off on.

Placing people's experience of freedom at the center of the discussion means beginning with an empirical observation, rather than a definition of freedom. The observation is that the way people, especially young people, seem to experience freedom does not translate readily into their own concepts of freedom. When asked to talk about experiences of freedom, people talk about sleeping, dreaming, sinking into a warm bath with a glass of wine, losing oneself in a good book, or stretching out on the sofa in the dark, after the rest of the family is asleep. Frequently but less often they talk about the experiences of good fellowship—relaxing with friends and with a beer. These are, of course, not the only experiences of freedom, but they are the leading ones. When asked to define freedom, however, people switched gears. In response to the simple question "What's freedom?" most people answered in terms of mastery, money, and power.

If people have experiences of freedom that don't readily fit into the familiar concepts, can we enlarge the concept in order to contain these experiences? Is there any danger in doing so, such as losing the normative force of the concept of freedom?[3] I do not imagine that I tap an original understanding of freedom prior to language when I ask about experiences of freedom, only that the stories people tell about their experiences with freedom are different from the stories that are philosophers' definitions of freedom, or even people's own definitions.

My approach runs the risk of metamorphosing the question, "What is freedom?" into the question, "What does it feel like to be free?" There is, however, an equal and opposite risk, that of writing as though definition and experience have nothing to do with each other. The latter path is not just the path of intellectual sterility. It is the path of political passivity and anger, as people are told they are free but don't feel it. This is the case with most of the young people I spoke with. My approach, which moves back and forth between experience and definition of freedom (people's own definitions as well as the definitions of several famous philosophers of freedom), takes no principled stand as to which is more fundamental—experience or definition. I assume only that experience and definition should be in constant contact. Here's the best course. Use the experience of freedom to question, challenge, and expand the concept of freedom. The concept need not be slave to experience, but it should not be the tyrant of experience either.

About the venerable problem of free will, I do not think it terribly important, but the issue cannot be excluded in advance. Free will is a metaphysical problem about which no empirical evidence can decide (Hampshire, 1975). Fortunately, it is not necessary to solve the problem of "free will" in order to make progress on the issue with which I am concerned, the disconnection between the experience of freedom and the concept of freedom. It is only necessary to understand that one's perspective on free will may be implicit in one's concept, and perhaps even in one's experience of freedom. If people think they have free will, they may experience freedom differently than if they don't. Whether people actually have free will is beyond the borders of this manuscript, concerning as it does an issue about which empirical evidence is of little relevance.

My position is not the same as John Stuart Mill (1975, 3), who begins the finest tract on freedom ever written, *On Liberty*, originally published in 1859, by saying that his subject is not "the so-called Liberty of the Will," but "Civil, or Social Liberty." On the contrary, if people believe that they have free will, this will affect how they understand their civil or social liberty, and this I am interested in. What I am not interested in is whether "free will" actually exists, as this is a metaphysical issue.

What People Said

I expected most people to be followers of Mill, naïve exponents of negative freedom, as it is often called, not because it is bad but because it is about removing negations to my freedom. Negative freedom is the freedom to be left alone to do what I want. Freedom means doing what I want unless it violates the rights of others. This is what I thought most Americans believed, as though Mill's "harm principle" were the first and last word on freedom. "The only purpose for which power can be rightfully exercised over any member of a civilised community, against his will, is to prevent harm to others" (Mill, 1975, 10–11).

This, the reader knows by now, is not what most people said.

Tarma, whose family emigrated from India, told of working as a grocery clerk in an expensive area of Washington, D.C. His family lived there, but most of the people who shopped at the local Safeway assumed otherwise, if they thought about it at all.

"They had the freedom to insult me, and I had the freedom to insult them back. That's what freedom's good for."

Did you ever try to talk with them about their attitudes, I asked?

"Sometimes. But that doesn't have anything to do with freedom does it? Freedom means they can say what they want, and I can say what I want."

And that is that, he might have added. Freedom is a low-level good, in some small way protecting his dignity. But, for Tarma, what really matters is that one day he will be rich and powerful enough to ignore them.

"I thought I'd get in trouble when I insulted the customers back, but no one ever complained. I didn't care if I got fired, but finally I realized that it doesn't matter what you say. No one cares. What matters is being powerful enough not to have to say anything. I talked back because I was weak."

Most people would be excited about freedom, I'd thought. Isn't freedom what the American dream is all about? It is for our freedom that we are fighting the terrorists. In fact, most people were not excited about freedom. Certainly part of this has to do with the fact that they have freedom in abundance; they assume freedom as their birthright. But there is another factor at work. Power not freedom is the real object of their desire.

What kind of world do young people live in, so that freedom tends to be seen as the realm of effete rights, such as freedom of speech, press, and assembly? Part of the answer is that they live in a world without history, in which everything they have they take for granted. Another part of the answer is that they live in a remarkably tolerant and hetero-geneous world, in which the social pressure about which Mill and Tocqueville were so concerned, what both called the "tyranny of the majority," is obscure to them (Mill, 1975, 6). With that term, both Mill and Tocqueville refer to informal social pressure to conform and fit in. Tocqueville's fable of the forest is a story about how this pressure can be at once both powerful and invisible, so internalized that it seems like reality itself.

"I have a right to do anything I want, anything that's legal anyhow," Tarma concludes. But I can't *do* anything I want. That takes more than freedom. Freedom is concerned with my rights. What I get to do with them depends on how much money and power I can get. That's why I'm in school.

Like Tarma, most people define freedom in negative terms (i.e., as lack of obstacles), but seem to regard it as relatively unimportant compared to what it takes to do what they want, above all "a lot of money." The fact that people assume that they should be able to do what they want, or at least there is a possibility that they can do what they want, reveals them to be naïve individualists.

Naïve individualism, not the worst thing in the world, should better be called frustrated naïve individualism. Most people expect to have what they fear they cannot have, power over their own lives. One might argue that most people I spoke with are young and naïve. They have grown up in a consumer society in which the commercial media panders to narcissistic fantasies of total control and a world without limits. Give them a few years, and they will learn how limited anyone's power really is. True enough, especially since older people don't equate power and freedom as openly. But as John Stuart Mill reminds us about freedom, even views we disagree with may help us articulate our own. Let's approach young people's views of freedom in this light.

How is it that slightly more than half of young people answer "no" to the question, "Is the United States a free country?" In part, of course, the answer is that they take their formal freedoms for granted. The other part of the answer is that they understand freedom in profoundly materialistic terms, which is another way of saying that they expect it to be real. And not just real, but complete and total. "If I'm not free to control every aspect of my life, then I'm not free." No one put it in quite these words, but this was the sense of freedom expressed by many.

About an experience with freedom, Amos is stumped. He can't think of anything to say. Finally, he says, "to stay within bounds and go as fast as I can. That's freedom." He is referring to his career, the way he expects to graduate early and begin medical school before his friends, the way he already knows what he is going to specialize in when he gets out. Later on he talks about freedom in terms of driving fast on a divided highway, no one else around. "Nothing touches me." What's clear in both cases is that freedom means moving as rapidly as possible in a direction that was laid out by someone else. His job is to follow quickly and well. Amos's father is a doctor, and that is what he always expected to be. Nor does he regret his destiny. Still, he wonders.

"I saw a story about Nadia Comaneci [a Rumanian gymnast who defected to the United States in 1989, and recently became a U.S. citizen]. She had all she wanted: money, a great house, she could travel. Sure, she couldn't disagree with her government, but who really cares about that? So why did she defect? She must have cared. I wonder what she wanted."

Amos paused before continuing with what seemed to be a new line of thought, but probably wasn't. "Sometimes I wish I could just stop for a year, drive across the country. Visit Europe. Some of my friends' parents did that. But today there's too much competition."

Amos does not quite fit the picture painted here. He comes closer to that drawn by David Brooks (2001) in "The Organization Kid," an article based on interviews with Princeton undergraduates. Like Amos, these organization kids are not discontented with their lack of freedom. They had evidently not expected to be free, just successful, the ones who would end up at the top of the heap.

Most young people interviewed will not be as successful as Amos will likely be. The result is that they are more troubled about their lack of freedom. Like Amos, they tend to equate power, money, and freedom. Unlike Amos, they already know they will probably not be among the power elite, as it used to be called. The result is not just bafflement but resentment. Many had expected to be free. This is what their schools and advertisements had taught them.

"Freedom makes me angry. Everyone says I'm free, only I don't feel free. I have loans to pay back, and a boss who thinks I don't work hard enough. My wife's sick and can't work, and our HMO won't let her see a specialist. I can't even take a vacation. On a good day it takes me an hour to drive to work. If I were free, I'd have more choices. I wouldn't feel so boxed in."

Is Dave simply wrong? Or is he expressing in an inchoate way the sense that the life he lives is dominated by forces over which he has no control—the forces of economics, bureaucracy, and experts? For Dave, as for many others, it is not the formal freedoms of speech, press, assembly, and religion that matter. What matters, what makes people angry and confused, is the fact that they don't feel free in their everyday lives because they lack control over their fates and choices, or at least they feel they do.

Though they feel boxed in, many people draw a sharp distinction between inner and outer freedom. "My cubicle at work is like a jail cell. My boss is a tyrant. But in a way it doesn't matter. I can think what I want about him, about work, about anything. In my mind I'm free."

Do you ever wish you were a little less free in your mind, and a little freer at work? I asked.

"I never thought of it that way," replied Sandra. "One doesn't really have much to do with the other, does it?"

This disconnection was the norm, though it turns out to be a complicated story. Most people seem to believe that inner freedom *shouldn't* have much to do with outer freedom: their separation is an ideal, not just a fact. Most people are, in other words, would-be stoics, desperate to preserve an inner realm of freedom from the intrusions of the world. At the same time, most people believe they are too weak to be true stoics, and so must pursue power and money, lest they end up with no freedom at all.

Other themes were common, particularly the concept of freedom as the ability to "cut out, leave, just walk out the door and not come back," as Henry put it.

"The ancient Greeks were freer than we are," continued Henry.

Why, I asked? Because the men could all participate in politics?

Henry looked at me blankly. "No, because they didn't have passports. They could just go where they wanted when they wanted. If they didn't like something, they could just leave."

Son of a high-level diplomat who had served all over the world, Henry knew a thing or two about passports. Still, it is worth wondering why a passport wouldn't be an icon of freedom (even the name suggests freedom), but a barrier, a limitation. The answer, evidently, is that a passport implies the existence of boundaries and limits. One can cross them, but that takes the permission of others, and that is no longer freedom.

Not having to ask permission turned out to be a leading example of freedom, mentioned by almost one-quarter of the people I talked with. It's a puzzling example, as though having to ask permission was a mark of weakness, and a sign of humiliation. At least this is how those who use having to ask permission as an example generally spoke about it: having to ask permission reveals the power differential between the parties, and it is the knowledge of that differential that is humiliating.

Dan, who runs a small business whose activities require the approval of a government agency, said, "I know they'll say yes. It's a rubber stamp, always has been. No one really cares. It just bugs me that I have to ask. They don't even make me wait. They just make me ask."

Does that make you less free?

"Absolutely. How can I be free if I have to ask first?"

Among the most famous works of the French philosopher Jean-Jacques Rousseau is *Emile: or On Education* (1979), a novel that imagines what the ideal education of an average young man named Emile might look like if the tutor could control every aspect of his student's life. Central to this education was that the tutor hide behind the curtain, so to speak, so that Emile never learns that it is other humans who thwart his desires. Instead, Emile "must be dependent on things and not on wills. The tutor and his helpers must disappear, as it were, and everything that happens to the child must seem to be an inevitable effect of nature" (Bloom, 1979, 11). If Emile were to learn that it was other humans who actually thwarted his will, he would be narcissistically injured, as we call it today—that is, suffer a wound to his self-esteem, and so become dependent on the opinions of others. Freedom for Rousseau means freedom from narcissistic injury, the enforced recognition that there are other wills more powerful than one's own.

For many people, freedom seems to have a similar meaning. One might argue that they are really talking about the experience of being crushed and constrained by bureaucracy, as with the case of Dave and his wife's HMO. Sometimes this is what people seem to be saying. Other times they are saying more than this, or less. Sometimes it is not abstract bureaucracy, but personal authority, indeed the mere otherness of others in positions of authority that is an insult to an informant's freedom. Or so it seemed to me.

Only two people talked about freedom in terms of political participation. In both cases that was with a loose-knit (what else?) group of anarchists, come together to protest the meetings of the World Trade Organization in Washington, D.C.

"We didn't march," said one. "We ran through the streets, a thousand black-masked anarchists. It was my greatest experience of freedom. For a little while we owned the city."

"I was part of a group without losing any of my individuality. I never felt like that before," said the other anarchist. "It was awesome."

The Distinction between Negative and Positive Freedom Doesn't Fit

The most striking thing about people's responses is that when asked a series of questions designed to elicit their working definitions of freedom, most don't seem to be answering in terms of freedom, at least as it is normally understood in the liberal (i.e., individualistic) democratic West. The philosopher who states this liberal, individualistic understanding most clearly is Isaiah Berlin, who died several years ago. In "Two Concepts of Liberty," Berlin (1969) argues that we should not confuse freedom with every good thing, such as a decent income and life chances. Everything is what it is, and not something else. Freedom means lack of restraint. Berlin calls it "negative liberty," not because it is bad, but because the definition focuses on limits to my actions. To know my freedom, says Berlin, I have but to ask how many doors are open to me, and how wide they are open. "The rest is extension of this sense, or else metaphor" (1969, lvi). (Like Berlin, I draw no distinction between liberty and freedom.)

Against negative liberty, Berlin sets "positive liberty," the freedom to realize one's deepest ambitions, to participate in one's own governance, and so become who one truly is. Under positive liberty, I am not free just because no one prevents me from speaking out in public or from getting a better education. Because positive liberty includes the means to realize my values, I am free only when I have the means to get others to listen to me (access to the Internet, e.g.), and only when I have a chance to get a decent education, what it takes to open doors in this world. Berlin worries that "positive liberty" risks giving too much power to the government, or even to my fellow citizens. For you to possess the means to self-development, such as a college education, I may have to be more heavily taxed, which restricts my freedom to travel, for example. How much more liberty do I really have, asks Berlin, when it is a majority of my fellow citizens, rather than the tyrant, who tell me what to do?

Most people's views of freedom don't readily fit into either negative or positive freedom. Certainly most people can be read as saying that they would be freer if they had more money and power. A lack of money and power are doors closed on their freedom. Seen from this perspective, most people's views can be reconciled with the category of negative freedom, but only by doing violence to what they are saying. One could also reconcile their views with positive freedom. Money and power are the essential means to self-realization, and so part of freedom itself. This too would do violence to what most people are saying.

People generally do not say that a lack of money and power prevents them from being free. They say that freedom is relatively unimportant compared to money and power. Freedom is effete; money and power are real. Many say this, it seems, because freedom has the quality of all or nothing: if they can't be completely free, then they want none of it, including none of the mere symbols of freedom, such as free speech, for this is how many regard such liberties.

For one with a background and interest in psychoanalytic theory, I could not help noticing that there was a borderline quality to many of the responses about freedom. The term "borderline quality" refers to what is called borderline personality disorder, though that puts it in terms too extreme. Not a borderline disorder, but a tendency toward the extremes of all or nothing characteristic of borderline thinking marked many of the responses. "If I am not free to do what I want in every aspect of my life, then not only am I not free, but freedom means nothing. What I want is power." This is a harsh, but not unfair, summary of the views of many of the younger people I talked with.

Theirs is a position not without its charms, a species of romantic materialism that will not be satisfied with empty promises and vague ideals. Freedom is real, concrete, and personal, or it is nothing. At first, I was terribly impressed with many young people's views of freedom. They had overcome the prevailing ideology of negative freedom, demanding instead that freedom be real, personal, and transformative, what Berlin calls positive freedom: not just a matter of open doors, but the ability to realize one's fullest potential. In their refusal to accept symbols of freedom for its substance, many young people were committed to a more radical and transcendent view of freedom than I ever imagined. Or so I thought during the first few months of interviews.

Gradually my interpretation changed. As I interviewed more young people, I was struck by the lack of imagination in many of the responses: not only did freedom have to be real or it was nothing, but real seemed to mean total control over every aspect of life. If my wife isn't referred to a medical specialist by my HMO, then I'm not free. Rarely did I hear anyone make distinctions like George did. "At work I'm a serf, but in the summer, when it's still light, and the kids and I can go bike riding after work . . . what king could have more freedom than that? I guess the difference is that kings get to have that feeling all the time. Still, sometimes I remember that feeling at work. That counts for something, doesn't it?"

It counts for a lot. Not just the feeling, but the emotional and intellectual subtlety to find freedom in the midst of an existence felt to be largely unfree, remembering moments of freedom during long periods of constraint and oppression, and so for a moment feeling free again. Few people talked like that.

Another who did was Rosa, who recently emigrated from a small town in Southern Mexico, the scene of revolutionary violence. As a child she slept under her bed to keep from getting accidentally shot; she couldn't go to school for several years. For Rosa, "freedom is going to school, having books and hot water." She's grateful to be living and working in the United States, but what she really longs for is to go home and live with her family in peace.

"Here I'm free to live in peace and security. I'm thankful, I really am. But it's not really freedom. Real freedom would be to have these things and live at home at the same time. Now I have to choose. Maybe someday . . ."

Rosa appreciates a limited freedom while longing for another, more complete freedom. It seems a simple achievement. In fact it's enormously sophisticated, so sophisticated she must contradict herself to say it. Most people were less sophisticated, their views of freedom having an all or nothing quality. In one respect that is admirable. Imagination can be more than a creative defense; it can be a lie, covering my chains with imaginary garlands of flowers. But this does not mean that freedom is best understood in the language of all or nothing.

Still, there is something in the literalism of many young people's views about freedom that fascinates. Consider Ronaldo, who likes to answer his own rhetorical questions. "Am I free? Well, I'm only working part time this summer. So most afternoons I'm free to get in my car and drive to the beach. That sounds like freedom, doesn't it? But, then I get to thinking about it, and I wonder. To get to the beach I have to go downstairs, get in my car, drive to the beach, obey the speed limits. The traffic is terrible. It takes me almost an hour to get there, and then the parking lot is full, so I have to drive around for fifteen minutes to find a space. Would you call that freedom? I don't."

And I don't know.

The Second Dimension of Freedom

The tendency among many young people is not just to see freedom in terms of power but also to see power in terms of all or nothing. Either I have it or I don't. Categories such as "enough power," "sufficient autonomy," or "some influence over my own life," were rare. Power becomes a zero-sum game, the currency of a world best described by Thomas Hobbes in *Leviathan*. Before there were governments, says Hobbes, men and women lived in a state of nature where life was nasty, brutish, mean, and short. In the state of nature, men must devote themselves to acquiring ever more power, lest it be taken from them. Power is the ultimate scarce resource: the more for you, the less for me. As Hobbes puts it,

> I put for a generall inclination of all mankind, a perpetuall and restlesse desire of Power after power, that ceaseth onely in Death. And the cause of this, is not always that a man hopes for a more intensive delight, than he has already attained to; or that he cannot be content with a moderate power: but because he cannot assure the power and means to live well, which he hath present, without the acquisition of more. (Hobbes, 1968, 161)

Though Hobbes's way of thinking dominates young people's waking hours, these same men and women express another way of thinking that, while not as dominant as the first, is present in the narratives of most. This theme generally emerged later in the interview, often in response to an invitation to "Tell me a story about freedom?" or "When are you most free?" I believe it was the more experiential quality of these questions, such as the invitation to tell a story, which evoked different answers. It might, however, have been that later in the interview people were more comfortable talking about what is in some ways an even more threatening experience of freedom: freedom as sleep, hot baths, relaxation, and letting go. The more intimidating and menacing the world, the more threatening these experiences of freedom are likely to be, as though one was lying down on the job, rendering oneself vulnerable to all the other wolves, as Hobbes calls them. For several interviews I switched the order of the questions in order to see if that made the difference. All in all, the quality of the question seemed to make more of a difference than the placement, but that is hard to tell. Likely it was both factors.

What was the most common experience of freedom in this second dimension? Two were equally popular. One was sleep, when the cares of the world, all the constraints and demands of the day, slip away, and one is free to just be, subject to a part of oneself kept under lock and key during the day, a part that sometimes surprises and delights with its dreams. Seven people went further, saying only in death would they be truly free. They did not seem particularly depressed, just driven to take their thoughts to their logical conclusion.

While listening to people talk about this aspect of freedom, the freedom of sleep, release, and for a few even death, I was reminded of the last dream of Alcibiades, the most fascinating of all the ancient Greeks. Would-be lover of Socrates, Alcibiades was beautiful and successful in every season of his life, which was devoted to being the best at everything, what the Greeks called *arête*, or excellence. The best at love, politics, warfare, and the Olympics, Alcibiades' life was an unbroken *agon*, the Greek term for struggle that comes down to us as agony. Shortly before his death at the hands of the brothers of some woman he took up with, Plutarch tells us that Alcibiades had a strange dream: that his mistress dressed him as a woman and put makeup on his face (*Lives*, 39). Alcibiades' dream was a dream of freedom—release from his agony, the perpetual struggle for excellence that was Alcibiades' life and death. For Alcibiades too, the freedom of struggle and mastery, including self-mastery, gave way to the freedom of passivity and submission. This is represented by Alcibiades' identification with a woman; especially at Athens, women were idealized for their silence, passivity, and submissiveness (Thucydides, *History*, 2.46).[4] It is something like this that many people want—the freedom of passivity and abandonment, a release not easily found in their worlds.

The other leading experience of freedom in this second dimension takes place at the end of the day, when one has met the demands of the day, or they must wait until tomorrow. A glass of wine, music, a hot bath, time to stretch out for a few minutes and think one's own thoughts, often in the darkness, when everyone else is asleep: that's freedom. Like sleep, this experience of relaxation was generally experienced as a type of letting go, losing control of oneself, or at least letting go of one's need to control the world. "I'm a control freak. But late at night, when everyone else is asleep, sometimes I can just let go and be myself for a little while." For Sally, being herself means to stop trying to control everyone else.

Far fewer people said morning was the time of day they were most free, but the reasoning was the same as those who said they were most free at night. "Early in the morning, before the phones start ringing, and no one is yelling 'Mom!' That's when I'm most free." Clara put it this way. "I think I'm most free in the morning. That way I start the day as an individual. Just me. During the day others come into my life, but in the morning it's just me."

More than a few said there was never a time of day they felt free, and the reasoning was always the same. "Every second I have to think about what I should be doing." Not even sleep was a respite.

While sleep and finding a space for oneself in the midst of a life filled with too many demands were the leading experiences of respite, another was relaxing with friends. It was a less common example, but not rare. Once again, the reasoning is almost always the same. "When I'm with my friends, I don't have to monitor myself. I can say anything, and they can say anything. That's freedom."

But can you really say anything, I asked, taking Laura a little too literally?

"No. I wouldn't want to hurt someone's feelings. But since I don't want to do that anyway, I'm free to say what I want."

Listening to Laura, one can appreciate Kant's view of freedom a little more. For Immanuel Kant, freedom is not about doing what I want to do. Kant calls that *Willkür*, or arbitrary will: acting on the desire of the moment. Real freedom is doing what I really want to do in the long run, what he calls *Wille*. Laura does not want to act in an arbitrary, willful fashion, so the freedom to do so would not be real freedom.

Generally, it was the same people who defined freedom in terms of mastery and money who talked of experiences of freedom in terms of sleep and relaxation. Frequently, they made no connection between these two experiences of freedom, as though they belonged to different worlds.

When people were asked if they saw any connection between these two experiences of freedom, many recognized that they might have something to do with each other, but few could put words to the connection. One who could said simply, "I think if I enjoyed my work more, then being at work would be more like relaxing at home after work. I wouldn't worry so much about moving up the ladder."

In fact, it was not quite so simple. Some people were not very good at making the connection with their words, but their stories about the place of freedom in their own lives seemed to do a better job. In other words, their narratives sounded as if they connected mastery and relaxation in their lives, even if they were not very articulate about how they did so. A couple of contrasting examples will help to explain this.

Consider Ronaldo again. Recently, he got into what he calls a "panic state" thinking about freedom. A few months ago he moved into his own apartment, and his time is his own. "That means I'm free. I think the panic stems from realizing that if I were totally free I'd be totally isolated."

Maybe you can be free with others, I said.

"No, I like being with others. I need them. But when I'm with them I have to compromise, and that means I'm not free."

Or consider Michael, who recently graduated from college, and is working as a temp. "I have a choice to make. Either I put on a suit and make money, and that means I lose my freedom, or I continue doing what I'm doing [he works a couple of days a week]. I've got the time, which means I've got my freedom. I just don't have the money, so my freedom's not much good, is it?"

Both Ronaldo and Michael equate freedom with being able to control their own time. It was a common equation, one that means that almost anything they do in a world with others is bound to subtract from their freedom. Neither can see any solution, which means they're stuck. Their experiences of freedom are split. Not, in this case, because they cannot talk about the connection between freedom as mastery and freedom as relaxation, for they do so better than many people, but because they can envisage no solution, no way of thinking about freedom, that might preserve or even enhance their freedom, as they enter into a world shared with others. One is alone and free, or with others and unfree.

Peter shares the same working assumption as Ronaldo and Michael. "Freedom is comfort and control over my own life."

What's the connection between comfort and control, I ask?

"When I have control, then I have comfort," Peter responds.

But, as Peter continues to talk about freedom, the boundaries between comfort, control, and freedom begin to blur. Unlike Ronaldo, he talks about freedom in terms of shared experiences with others, experiences that seem to enhance rather than threaten his freedom.

Tell me about an experience of freedom, I asked.

"I met a friend downtown for lunch. We ate. He had to go back to the office for a little while. I had the afternoon off, so I bought a magazine and read it in the park. He met up with me later, and we walked to a hill overlooking the Potomac. He'd brought a bottle of wine; we sat and watched the river and talked about our lives. Afterward I felt good, like I'd worked out at the gym."

When I asked Peter when he felt most free, his answer was again in terms of the comfort he feels when he is with friends. Rarely did he talk about freedom in terms of mastery, even though he had defined freedom as the comfort that stems from mastery. For Peter, freedom as mastery seems more cultural baggage than felt experience, even as it is hard to distinguish the two.

Most people I spoke with (a bare majority) come a little closer to Peter than Ronaldo and Michael. Not necessarily because most people split freedom less, for they don't, but because they are not quite as stuck as Ronaldo and Michael. In other words, most people's narratives of freedom are about as split as Ronaldo's and Michael's, but their lives seem to be a little more imaginative and flexible, indeed freer, than their concepts would allow. But only a little.

There is no easy way to summarize this second dimension of freedom, so split off from the first for most people. If one had to put a name to it, the best would be Epicurean freedom. The term "Epicurean" is today utterly misleading, referring as it does to someone who likes fine wine, good food, and the like. For the original followers of Epicurus, the goal was to live a simple life, free of pain, stress, and the desire for things that one cannot readily have. Only such a simple life was free, because such a life allows the individual to experience his own existence, liberated from the desire for every new thing.

> The state of equilibrium . . . makes the individual conscious of a global, coenesthetic feeling of his own existence. It is as though . . . he was finally free to become aware of something extraordinary, already present in him unconsciously: the pleasure of his own existence, or (in Diano's words) of "the identity of pure existence." (Hadot, 2002, 116)

Freedom, from this perspective, is not about the fulfillment of desire, but desire's cessation. One doesn't need much, and so one has all one needs. The result is that one is finally free to just be.

Like the original Epicureans, many people experience this pleasure not just in sleep and retreat but also in discussion and the pleasures of friendship, even if few seek the supreme Epicurean pleasure of contemplating the infinity of the gods.

Unlike the Stoic, the Epicurean sought the reformulation not the suppression of desire, so that one is content with goods relatively easy to obtain: simple foods and clothes, while renouncing wealth, honors, and public positions, all the while living in retreat. Not in isolation, however; friendship remains a distinctly human satisfaction. Seen from this perspective, it would be more accurate to say that most people are wanna-be Epicureans, wishing they could be satisfied with simple pleasures, but knowing that they cannot. The pull of conventional definitions of success is too strong, their imagination for alternatives too weak. The result is that Epicureanism becomes for most a pleasure of the night, a split-off satisfaction, but for this reason no less important, even if it is generally unavailable to challenge conventional definitions of success and freedom.

This is how I would answer a reader who said something like the following. "You know, the division of freedom into mastery and respite is not necessarily evidence of a split experience of freedom. These are simply two dimensions of any full-fledged experience of freedom: freedom as activity, including mastery, and freedom as passivity, including abandoning oneself to experience." There would be some truth to such criticism, but only some. The problem is not that people talk about two different aspects of freedom. The problem is that most people cannot put these two experiences of freedom together, talking instead as if they belonged to separate worlds that never touch. For most people, not only do experiences of freedom in the realm of dreams and imagination have nothing to do with freedom as it is lived in everyday life, but most people talk as if they expect (even hope) that there should be no connection, as though everyday life has the power to crush every hope and dream. In other words, the second dimension of freedom generates no critique of the first, and only brief respite from it. It is in this vein that I turn to Sartre and Marcuse in later chapters.

Do People Lack the Concepts to Explain Their Experiences?

Among social theorists it is widely held that average people lack the concepts and ideological sophistication to make sense of their own experiences. Once this was called false-consciousness. For example, in *Habits of the Heart*, a study of the place of community in Americans' lives, Robert Bellah et al. (1985) argue that Americans lack the cultural concepts to make sense of their own desires for community. Many Americans want to sacrifice, to give of themselves to others, but little in this individualistic, acquisitive culture helps them put words to this desire. The result is that they are confused about what they want.

In a similar vein, Jennifer Hochschild in *What's Fair?* (1981, 255) refers to Antonio Gramsci's "two consciousnesses," in which what appears to be ambivalence and even incoherence is actually a type of ideological blindness, as one lacks the concepts to say what one's experience is. This, Hochschild believes, explains the way so many of her subjects talked about equality: they have been taught that inequality is necessary, even good, but their experiences incline them toward redistribution, at least in some cases. "As a result, they feel hesitant, confused, and anxious, and may appear to be inconsistent and nonideological." (Hochschild's book was an inspiration for my own, particularly the way she uses qualitative research to reinterpret large quantitative studies of what people say they believe about fairness.)

The people I talked with exhibit two consciousnesses about freedom.

Consciousness one: a definition of freedom that is positive and personal. Freedom means doing what I want in every aspect of my life. That takes mastery and money. Associated with this view is contempt for such effete freedoms as speech, indeed for political freedom in general.

Consciousness two: experiences of freedom that don't fit the mastery and money model, experiences of relaxation, generally alone, after the day is done, but frequently in the company of friends.

Neither of these consciousnesses is political. For Gramsci that would be a problem. For me too, though I would put it a little differently. The problem is not that most people lack a politically astute view of freedom, as though ideological sophistication were a value in itself. The problem is that people are unlikely to become as free as they might because they fail to understand how their freedom is involved with that of others.

This might seem to be the same point expressed in two different ways, and perhaps it is. The difference is that unlike Gramsci, my version explicitly makes the individual's freedom the highest value; ideological clarity is valuable only to the degree with which it serves that goal. From this perspective, consciousness one (freedom as mastery) is not so much ideologically deficient as practically uninformed. As a matter of fact, most people will not achieve the mastery they seek except in association with others. When they do this, they may find that mastery and relaxation belong to worlds not quite so far apart. This is probably as good as it gets.

Does this mean that I too believe that most people lack the concepts to explain their own experiences with freedom? Yes and no. People's views about freedom are split because the reality they live in is similarly split. The split in informants' views about freedom (i.e., the split between freedom as mastery and freedom as respite) reflects a realistic perception of the world, which is also split. The economic world they live in really is harsh, competitive, and relatively unforgiving, like Hobbes's state of nature. If you lose your job and can't find another, you and your spouse will likely lose your health insurance (if you are fortunate enough to be insured in the first place), and so will your children. Someone could get sick and die, especially if he or she has a chronic condition not readily treated in the emergency room, which must accept anyone, at least in theory. Death is not a likely outcome of economic failure in the United States, but it's possible, and most people know this. We should be careful about expecting people to integrate the two dimensions of freedom in their minds when they are not readily integrated in reality. That would not be true-consciousness, but idealism.

The relationship between inner world and external reality is extraordinarily complex and subtle; it is almost impossible to give both their due. For now it must suffice to say that while there is something in the nature of the experience of freedom itself that lends itself to splitting, the extent of the split of one's experience of freedom depends greatly upon the society in which the individual lives. A person with a modest tendency toward borderline thinking about freedom (this includes most people) will experience this tendency in exaggerated form in a society like our own. This is the topic of the next chapter, and while the point may seem obvious, it is important, for it is not my argument that societies and cultures live a life of their own. To say that ours is a culture in which freedom is experienced in borderline terms means that the individuals in that culture tend, as a group, but counted one by one, to see the world in this way. In other words, I adhere to methodological individualism, even as I refer to cultural tendencies.

As they live their lives everyday, the people I spoke with experience a world in which everything is for sale, including freedom. By freedom they mean not just the freedom to retire at 30 to South Beach but also the freedom to see a medical specialist. It would be an intellectual's conceit to imagine that the split in freedom that marks young people's discussions could be healed by providing them with a more subtle and sophisticated vocabulary of freedom. New ways of living are needed not new words.

For a few people, often but not always older, the second dimension of freedom—freedom as relaxation and letting go—was the leading theme, not an alternative to the struggle for mastery and money but an ideal way of life in itself. For Ellen, "freedom means losing myself in a book, or going to a play and sitting in the front row, and becoming part of the drama."

Why is this so important to you, I asked?

"Because if I couldn't do that, I'd feel trapped in myself."

Richard talked about freedom in terms of giving himself over to love of his wife, his family, to romance. "Falling in love with my wife all over again. That's freedom for me." "Falling in love" is a marvelous term, and just right. We have to give ourselves over to some experiences in order to have them. Freedom seems to be one.

Perhaps the most surprising account of freedom was Bob's, who defined freedom by telling a story about apologizing to a jerk at work. It made life easier on the job, where he had to deal with the jerk everyday, and the jerk wasn't really a bad guy, just an excitable one.

What's that got to do with freedom, I asked?

"By apologizing, even when I wasn't wrong, I created an atmosphere of harmony between us. Work goes better, and I'm more relaxed."

When I told Bob that he was one of the few people I talked with who didn't use the language of mastery when talking about freedom, he implied that I was wrong. "Right now I'm doing exactly what I want to. When I feel the organic unity of my life, then I don't have to get into pissing contests with people."

Rather than not equating freedom and mastery, Bob seems to be saying that he already has a type of mastery, and thus can pursue relaxation even in his relationships at work. That's a type of integration I had not counted on. Indeed, it is one of my regrets that in characterizing people's accounts of freedom in terms of a split between mastery and respite I must neglect the rich complexity of several individuals' resolutions of the conflict.

CHAPTER 2

BORDERLINES OF FREEDOM

Borderline personality disorder, a psychological diagnosis, best explains why young people experience freedom as they do. This claim may shock the reader. Borderline personality disorder is a severe mental illness. How can it be used to explain how a group of apparently normal people experience freedom? The answer, to put it briefly, is that I use the term "borderline personality disorder" much as Christopher Lasch (1979) used the term "narcissism" in *The Culture of Narcissism*, his indictment of the self-obsessed culture of the 1970s. "Borderline" is a cultural not just a psychological diagnosis. Since this distinction is not obvious, I will explain it along the way.

In "What's Wrong with Negative Liberty," Charles Taylor (1979, 176) argues that we need a more subtle and sophisticated moral psychology of freedom. "The moral psychology of these authors is too simple, or perhaps we should say too crude, for its purposes," says Taylor. He is referring not just to Thomas Hobbes, but to all who fail to recognize the ways in which fear and false-consciousness may stand in the way of freedom.

What follows is an attempt to develop a more subtle moral psychology of freedom. Though the attempt draws upon a sophisticated psychological concept to do so, what makes mine a study in moral psychology is not just the theory employed but the research method: in-depth interviews, averaging about an hour long, with 52 people. Although it was not a clinical interview, I nonetheless spent enough time with each person to develop a sense of his or her moral psychology of freedom—that is, the role that freedom plays in the story that is the subject's life, as told to me in the course of an interview.

A striking aspect of most stories was the way people defined freedom as mastery and money, but talked about experiences of freedom in terms of relaxation and respite. This led me to conclude that there was a split in people's experience of freedom, a split that is indwelling (i.e., inherent in the experience of freedom itself), even as it is exaggerated by the world we live in. Because this split finds its tally in the world, people cannot heal it themselves. Some people can, however, become more aware of this split, lessening the distance between mastery and respite just a little bit. That is probably as good as it gets, and as good as it should get. For political if not psychological reasons, some tension between mastery and respite is desirable. The political reasons are discussed in chapters 6 and 7.

Calling people's experience of freedom split refers to the schizoid process of dividing experience in two. Schizoid means split. Splitting is not the same as repression, in which I deny the existence or relevance of threatening experiences. In splitting I don't deny the experience, but I reject its connection to other experiences. Repression is based on a vertical model of the mind, in which one thing is put beneath another, so that I can't know it. Splitting is a horizontal model, different experiences held in separate watertight compartments. How watertight these compartments actually are varies considerably among the people I talked with, as chapter 1 tried to convey.

Splitting is the first psychological defense, the one that comes before other, more sophisticated defenses, such as denial, which frequently draw upon the developed ego. Borderline personality disorder is marked by its heavy use of splitting, and that is what brought it to mind while listening to the way many people talk about freedom.

It remains a big leap from talking about some surprising and disturbing characteristics of people's views of freedom to the conclusion that these exhibit borderline thinking. Certainly the men and women interviewed were not (as far as I could tell) ill in any clinical sense. If there is any illness around, it is in the society. To label their views of freedom "borderline," it is necessary to make the translation from a clinical to a cultural diagnosis.

The characterization of borderline personality disorder in the *Diagnostic and Statistical Manual of Mental Disorders* of the American Psychiatric Association (1994, 654; hereafter referred to as *DSM*) is not too helpful, seeing borderline personality disorder in terms too extreme, calling it "a pervasive pattern of instability in interpersonal relationships, self-image, and affects, and marked impulsivity beginning by early adulthood and present in a variety of contexts."

Originally, borderline meant being on the borderline between neurosis and psychosis. Nevertheless, Freud's remark that the neurotic is like the rest of us, only more so, applies to people suffering from borderline personality disorder as well. The difference between them and us, including the people I talked with, is one of degree.

The trait associated with borderline personality disorder most relevant to informants' concepts of freedom is the tendency to go toward extremes, such as "a pattern of unstable and intense interpersonal relationships characterized by alternating between extremes of idealization and devaluation" (*DSM IV*, 1994, 654). Borderline experience is marked by a division of the world into all and nothing at all. Do not some of our culture's ideal images of freedom, such as living in a world without boundaries or limits, free of all entanglements and obligations, able to do anything one wants, reflect borderline experience? "No boundaries" is the advertising slogan of the American Express credit card.

More helpful is Otto Kernberg's (1985) characterization of borderline experience in terms of the predominance of primitive defenses. Probably the single most well-known theorist of borderline personality disorder, Kernberg explains borderline experience in terms of the ego's most primitive defense, splitting, which divides the world in two. This would account for the leading attribute of borderline experience, the tendency toward extremes of idealization and devaluation. "If I am not completely free, then freedom is meaningless, and I might as well be in chains. So give me power instead." Though no one put it in quite these words, many came close to this way of thinking, one marked by a borderline quality characterized by the division of freedom into all or nothing at all.

Though Kernberg does not mention it, the reduction of relationships to that most primitive currency, money and power, fits his characterization of borderline experience as lacking the gift of imagination, one that can bridge the gap between presence and absence, all or nothing, by conjuring up an image of an absent person, place, or ideal. Deprived of imagination, which finds symbolic sources of comfort and satisfaction in the absence of the real thing (a letter in place of a person, or a memory of freedom in the midst of an oppressive existence), the power to get what one wants becomes the only value. In the case of freedom, the tendency to devalue its "symbolic" expressions, such as freedom of speech, press, and assembly, as unreal compared to power would have a borderline quality.

To be sure, it is possible to err in both directions. Young people's inability or refusal (I'm still not sure which) to find much comfort in symbols of freedom in the absence of its substance was in some ways refreshing, as though they wouldn't be satisfied by anything less than the real thing. Still, their inability to find any meaning in "mere symbols" remains troubling.

At about this point, the reader may be asking him or herself whether it really makes sense to characterize a cultural tendency in terms of a psychiatric disorder, especially one as severe as borderline personality disorder. The answer is that it makes as much sense as Christopher Lasch's (1979) characterization of American culture as a culture of narcissism. In fact, the connection is more than methodological or epistemological; it is substantive. What American psychiatrists and psychoanalysts call narcissism, British object relations theorists call schizoid.

> The term "narcissism" tends to be employed diagnostically by those proclaiming loyalty to the drive model (Kernberg) . . . "Schizoid" tends to be employed diagnostically by adherents of relational models (Fairbairn, Guntrip), who are interested in articulating their break with drive theory . . . These two differing diagnoses and accompanying formulations are applied to patients who are essentially similar, by theorists who start with very different conceptual premises and ideological affiliations. (Greenberg and Mitchell, 1983, 385)

Since borderline personality disorder is one of the most extreme forms of schizoid personality disorders, defined in terms of the predominance of primitive splitting defenses, it makes conceptual sense to say that there is a connection between the way of thinking about freedom that I call borderline and what Lasch called a culture of narcissism.

For Lasch, the culture of narcissism is a culture of control, achieved by shrinking one's world until it is compact enough to be mastered. That's what makes it narcissistic, the reduction of one's world to a size that is subject to total control. For most of us, this is a tiny world indeed.

If there are similarities between Lasch's culture of narcissism and the culture of the borderline (at least as far as freedom is concerned), there are differences as well. Disappointed grandiosity, the experience of most young people, is not the same thing as hidden grandiosity. Narcissists must hide their grandiosity, often even from themselves, lest it wilt in the light of day. Disappointed grandiosity has seen the light. The devaluation of formal freedoms, such as the Bill of Rights (what several young people refer to as mere symbols of freedom), is narcissistic, in so far as these symbols are not about me and my freedom right now. However, the mastery that most young people seek is not idealized as much as it is regretted, as though there were no other choice. Nor did most informants seem filled with rage, a signature of narcissistic personality disorder. Not suppressed rage, but disappointment, regret, and resentment come closer to the mark, and these are not readily experienced by narcissists, as these emotions are too complex and subtle. Regret, in particular, is not part of the language of narcissism. Rage, though, is a complicated story, and in chapter 3, I reflect on its possible permutation into cynicism in a number of informants.

Another difference between Lasch's account and my own is methodological. Unlike Lasch, I rely on extended interviews, which, while far from clinical, provide an opportunity to learn about the thinking, and sometimes feeling, that underlies people's willingness to substitute power for freedom. Implicit in the conversation of at least some I spoke with is a tone of regret. They wish they did not have to trade freedom for power, but dare not refuse, lest they end up with neither. Finally, the reader may be wondering if it is not I who am forcing people's experiences into binary categories, creating the phenomenon of borderline thinking that I subsequently discover. There is no way I can prove to the reader, or even to myself, that this is not so. And to some degree, at least, this must always be the case. One cannot discover what one is not, at least, prepared to experience. Certainly my quotations are selective as they must be, lest my manuscript become little more than hundreds of pages of transcripts.

Perhaps the best answer to the claim that I created the categories I discover is that these interviews were, in their own way, as difficult as the interviews I undertook with imprisoned murderers and rapists for a book on evil (Alford, 1997). Often, I felt torn listening to people talk about their experiences of freedom. During many interviews I felt that I couldn't put the pieces together, that the informant was using the term freedom in ways that seemed contradictory and counterintuitive, even to the informant.

If one trusts the countertransference, as it is called by psychoanalysts, then my experience too is evidence. Under the countertransference, the analyst feels the alienated and unintegrated experiences of the analysand, as though these experiences were lodged in the analyst, or as though these experiences belonged to no one but were located in the space between them, the inter-person. My interviews were hardly analytic sessions, but the countertransference is not confined to the analytic hour. It happens every time we are in a group, or with an individual, and experience feelings that seem not quite our own, but not truly other. I believe that the uneasiness I experienced in many interviews, the feeling that the informant was talking about experiences of freedom that just didn't add up, is itself evidence that I did not merely create what I discovered. Rather, I discovered what was created in me by those I spoke with. My experiences were their way of communicating what they could hardly put into words.

Finally, there were the relatively rare but for that reason especially striking interviews that did not fit the schizoid pattern I have described but instead felt whole, the elements of freedom integrated in a coherent pattern. The informant was not divided and neither was my experience of the interview. I don't think I would have been able to figure out what was so odd about most interviews without the occasional contrasting experience of interviews that did not fit the pattern, but revealed it by contrast. Along the way I give more examples of both pattern and contrast.

Losing, Fusing, and "In the Groove"

The most useful way of thinking about borderline experience is that of Roger Lewin and Clarence Schulz (1992) in *Losing and Fusing: Borderline Transitional Object and Self Relations*, which explores what it is that borderline experience lacks. Borderline experience lacks the gift of illusion, the ability to use imaginary creations, such as fantasies, illusions, and art, to modulate the swings between losing and fusing. In other words, borderline is the tendency to alternatively feel abandoned or engulfed, the tendency to oscillate between the poles, unable to use symbols and myths, such as a photo of a loved one or a favorite story about one's beloved, to buffer the oscillations. "When you're gone you don't exist; when you're here, nothing else exists, not even me." When borderline experience speaks, this is what it says.

Borderline experience reflects an inability to use what the analyst D. W. Winnicott calls transitional objects. By transitional object, Winnicott (1971a) means an object that is neither me nor not me but both and neither. The teddy bear or favorite blanket is often the child's first transitional object, but transitional objects are not just for children. Culture is the transitional object par excellence. Culture makes no sense if it is not part of me. But if it were only in me, culture would be no more than an illusion. Culture is me and not me at the same time, and sometimes it is best not to ask where to draw the line.

Illusion is the medium of transitional experience. Key to illusion is the way in which it resides in a realm between me and not me—neither inner nor outer. "I create it because it exists without me, but I won't be able to sustain this illusion if you keep asking me about it." If the psycho-logic of transitional experience spoke in sentences, this would be one. Illusion connects and separates internal and external reality, reflecting a separation from reality that is also a fusion with it. In this way, illusion buffers the swings between losing and fusing, the swings that—when they are extreme—mark borderline experience. Recall, by contrast, the way many people talked about internal and external freedom as though they had almost nothing to do with each other. Such a view cannot sustain the illusion necessary for transitional thinking.

Of course, one should not idealize illusion. False consciousness is also an illusion. What marks the illusion of transitional experience is the way in which it participates in the world, joining and separating us from the world at the same time. Freedom is not just an absence of constraint. Freedom is imagination, the ability to imagine oneself as resident of a material present, enriched but not distorted by the imagination. The sacred is exemplary, the mundane everyday world enriched by its participation in the transcendent, and so occasionally becoming numinous. For only a few does freedom remain sacred in this sense.

From time to time I will refer to the illusion of freedom, or say that freedom takes a little magic. By this I refer not to what is commonly called fantasy, but to the ability to use the resources of culture, such as books, music, and movies, to make the present reality shine with new possibilities, if only for a moment. In its own way, culture (and not just high culture) too is sacred, enriching mundane life with a glimpse of infinite possibility before returning us to the world. The ability to use culture in this way is itself a gift, one that many young people are lacking, at least as far as freedom is concerned.

In response to the obvious objection that this way of thinking about freedom only fosters the worst aspects of idealism, I remind the reader that it was no less a radical than Herbert Marcuse (1978) who saw in high bourgeois art a promise of liberation found nowhere else. I turn to this aspect of Marcuse's work in chapter 4, concluding with his explanation of why so many people are unable to use illusion. Not the illusory belief in a freedom that does not exist, but the inability to use illusion in order to become a little freer is today the greater danger.

Imagining that one is free while slaving away in a little cubicle may become false-consciousness, but the way in which this seems most likely to happen today is not that envisioned by George Orwell (1949) in his novel, *Nineteen Eighty-Four*. In Oceania, meaning is turned upside down, as the masses are led to chant such slogans as, "War is Peace" and "Freedom is Slavery." Today, ideology works in more subtle ways.

The way in which false-consciousness is most likely to express itself today is through citizens who can see no connection, and expect to see no connection, between the freedom of their imaginations and the freedom of everyday life. Imagining that one is free generates no critique of one's actual unfreedom, as one cannot imagine that there is a connection between mind and world, imagination and practice. The world is too massive and concrete for that. This is the way false-consciousness, if that term is still useful, seems to work in the people I talked with, coming closer to what Max Weber called rationalization: the world emptied of every illusion including that of freedom. What Winnicott calls transitional space, the realm of reality between me and not me, the realm partly formed by my imagination, is today parceled out between the realms of mind and material practice, with no connection between them. This is what marks borderline thinking.

In the late 1980s, the conservative philosopher Alan Bloom (1998) published the most unlikely bestseller in years, *The Closing of the American Mind.* Organized around his experience of teaching undergraduates at the University of Chicago, Bloom argued that mass entertainment, drugs, and a comfortable living have combined to convince young people that the world is divided in two: work and drudgery on the one hand, excitement, stimulation, and easy ecstasy on the other. The purpose of a liberal education is to convince young people that this is not true, that through study and hard work the cultivated imagination may inform the practice of everyday life, enriching both. My concern is similar—not that the imaginations of young people have atrophied, but that they do not expect their imaginations to have any influence on the world, or the world on their imaginations. Rather, imagination and material reality belong to separate categories of existence that never meet, which is another way of saying that the realm of illusion has fled. There is no magic left. Freedom takes a little magic.

Let's call this magic "freedom with." Jazz musicians talk about being "in the groove," a state of improvisation that involves not just me and my music but others as well if I am playing in a group. Although individual skills and talent are involved, they do not create the groove. The groove is created by the space among the players, not too close and not too tight. As such, "in the groove" is a temporary creation, as transient as the performance; the negotiation of talents it has been called, each player in tune with himself, the music, and the other players—at least for a little while.

"In the groove" expresses a spontaneity built on hundreds of hours of negotiation, learning to barter the assertion of others with one's own self-assertion. The negotiation of wills it might be called, except that it is not just will but will merged with talent to create something new. Intersubjectively warranted will it might be called. This sounds a little like that experience of positive freedom that Berlin condemns, in which I internalize the constraints of others and call it freedom. Whether this is bad depends, it seems, on what one is internalizing, a distinction Berlin recognizes when he calls attention to the difference between internalizing a piece of music and internalizing a doctrine. The former I can make my own; the latter almost always remains an alien presence (Berlin, 1969, 141). "In the groove" is, of course, not just an account of playing jazz music. It is a metaphor for the type of human relatedness associated with "freedom with."

"Freedom with" shares Winnicott's insight that the free person is one lucky enough to need others without being constantly reminded of this fact. "Freedom with" is the paradox of needing and using others in order not to be dependent upon them. As such, "freedom with" has the quality of what Winnicott calls a transitional relationship. "By flight to split-off intellectual functioning it is possible to resolve the paradox," says Winnicott, "but the price of this is the loss of the value of the paradox itself" (Winnicott, 1971b, xii).

The reader may not be convinced, especially if he or she is as harshly realistic as the people I spoke with. Every negotiation is a compromise, and in that sense at least the negotiation of talents is a loss of freedom. This is true, though, only from a perspective that equates freedom with the will. Living in a world of others requires the loss of the illusion that equates sovereign will with freedom. A student of Winnicott describes disillusionment in this way.

> After initial experience of need gratification from a good enough mother, when additional needs arise, the infant develops the illusion that he "created" his object of fulfillment . . . With the inevitable gradual disillusionment which occurs, transitional objects and phenomena appear as substitute satisfactions. They are created by the child's adaptation of a part of the external world to conform to the configurations of his needs. Since our needs are never completely satisfied, we are everlastingly preoccupied with attempts to adapt outer reality to inner need and express this in such "intermediate" forms of adult activity as artistic creativity. (Greenbaum, 1978, 195)

From this perspective, freedom comes awfully close to art. Freedom is the art of not always asking whether I am conforming to the world or the world is conforming to me. One can see how this would be invaluable in such musical experiences as "in the groove." If I were to ask whether the other musicians were following my will or whether I was following theirs, I would lose the experience.

To be sure, "freedom with" is risky business. Not asking who is conforming to whom may be an invitation to false-consciousness. Sometimes we should ask. On the other hand, the problem with positive freedom is not that it doesn't ask but that the answer is always the same: there is no difference between my enlightened will and that of the community, reason, or history. This is what rightly worries Berlin: that I will call freedom whatever limits and constrains me. It sounds odd, but there is something about the experience of freedom that lends itself to the equation of freedom with constraint. Exemplary is Jean-Jacques Rousseau's famous claim that whoever does not obey the General Will, by which he means the agreement of one's fellow citizens on the principles of society, shall be "forced to be free."

A striking contemporary example of this strange affinity of freedom for constraint is an advertisement for "Eye Promise"—a computer software that reports on all the Internet sites one has visited to an "accountability partner." The ad declares in bold headlines, "You'll Like the Feeling that You're Free to Surf!!!" A testimonial from a satisfied user reads, "It was incredible! It was totally freeing!" It sounds like the satisfied user had actually gone surfing in Maui, instead of signing up for a service that tracks his every move on the World Wide Web, so that he will be better able to resist temptation to view pornography or gamble on the Internet. You might imagine that this software was designed for parents to keep an eye on their children. In fact, it is marketed under the auspices of Promise Keepers, a Christian men's organization, and most of the testimonials and the examples refer to men keeping an eye on themselves (or rather, having other men do it for them), not on their children.[1]

What is it about freedom that gives it this strange affinity for constraint? Why would some people not only pay to subject themselves to this Eye, but find it liberating? Because finding the place and space called "freedom with" is difficult. Freedom has an affinity for the borderlines of losing and fusing. Many of us (and not just Promise Keepers) are more comfortable having someone else keep us far from the borderlines. Or rather, the presence of another who promises to keep us in line is experienced as freedom, as one is liberated from the harsh constraint of having to do it oneself. As Freud (1961, 92) reminds us, one's own superego, or conscience, is almost always the harshest critic of all. Indeed, this experience of self-punishment is the source of what Freud calls the discontent of civilization. To be disciplined by others may be such a relief that for a moment it feels like freedom.

There are better ways to experience freedom, ways that come closer to "freedom with." One way is to refuse to answer the question "Are you free?"

"Well, sometimes, when I'm driving my car, listening to music with the windows down, or just dreaming about going to London, then I feel free," replied Martia.

But are you really free, I persisted?

"I don't know, but it's just as good. To be truly, completely free I'd have not to be dependent on anyone. But then I'd be lonely. This is just as good."

Martia knows something about "freedom with" that I hadn't quite grasped. That one doesn't always have to know the difference between the experience and the definition, that sometimes the experience is the definition, or better.

Gregory, only a little older than the youngest informant, said that he used to feel free when driving over the Bay Bridge, a high span several miles long over the Chesapeake Bay connecting the eastern and western shores of Maryland. Last time he drove across the bridge it was different. He started thinking about all the people who designed and made the bridge. "Then I realized. It's only human hands that keep my car from falling into the ocean."

Did that make you feel less free, I asked?

"No, just different, like my freedom depended on others doing their work, so that the rivets don't fall out or something."

Not only is a bridge a non-borderline symbol of freedom (it connects the shores, the poles), but to imagine that this steel thing is actually the product of human hands is to know how much we depend on each other. To know this and still feel free is an act of creative imagination and wonder. What is not quite so clear is whether thinking of the Bay Bridge as a bridge of hands eased what was evidently a fairly strong phobic reaction to driving over the bridge, or whether it was the cause. Perhaps both.[2]

By its very nature, "freedom with" is a limited experience of freedom, found in between and alongside of the more dramatic moments of our lives, not in the midst of romantic passion but in its recollection. The singer Donovan sings that he rarely thinks of freedom without thinking of the times he has been loved. The tone of "Colours" is reverie, his memories segueing from the blond hair of the girl he loved to the blue color of the sky to the green color of the corn. He is alone, but he's not, and in this in-between state of reverie he can feel his freedom, connected to the world but separate at the same time, lightly held by remembered love.

Donovan's freedom is not an oceanic feeling that Freud (1961, 11) writes of; nor is it an experience of merger. Nor is Donovan's freedom "just another word for nothing left to lose," to mix popular songs for a moment. Donovan's freedom exists in some in-between place and time, most akin perhaps to what Winnicott calls being alone with another. In this state we do not pretend the other does not exist, or that we have no need of others. That is not freedom; that is avoidant attachment. Nor do we cling to other people or ideas. But we don't work at not clinging either. Donovan's freedom has the quality of being lightly held, so lightly that one can imagine being alone in the universe all the while knowing one is not. "Freedom with" is being lightly held.

Winnicott (1986) goes further, arguing that

The enjoyment of freedom only applies at all simply to the periods between bodily excitements. There is but little bodily gratification, and none that is acute, to be got out of freedom; whereas the ideas of cruelty or slavery are notoriously associated with bodily excitement and sensual experiences . . . Therefore, lovers of freedom must be expected periodically to feel the seductive power of the idea of slavery and control. (214)

This does not seem quite right. Certainly, the relaxation that many people equate with freedom has a sensuous quality, even if it is not "acute." Nevertheless, Winnicott is onto something. The pursuit of pleasure, as observers from Socrates to Sophocles and beyond have pointed out, often has a driven quality that is adverse to freedom.

Writing about the same time as Winnicott, the psychoanalyst Joseph Smith (1978, 96) defines freedom as "freedom from the compelling pressure of peremptory need" that is "nevertheless shaped by such needs." Freedom isn't liberation from need, as in having all I want or no longer wanting anything. Freedom is relief from the tension of tyrannical need that nonetheless remains under the impress of that need. The play we call freedom "sustains a dramatic quality," as our needs hover in the wings. In this regard, Smith adds complexity to Winnicott's statement that freedom applies "simply" to the periods between bodily excitement. There is nothing simple about it. Freedom performs on a stage in which the needs that excite us are just resting between acts. That experience gives freedom its edge.

What links Smith and Winnicott is their shared sense that attunement to and dependence on others and the external world, above all the world of symbols and values, actually liberates us from being enslaved by our desires (Smith, 1978, 97). Freedom is not the absence or rejection of need. Freedom is the liberation from need, which itself presumes the partial fulfillment of need. Because there once was enough, one need not devour it all. Because we were once totally dependent on others without being constantly reminded of this fact, we can tolerate our real dependence without aspiring to an autonomy that does not exist.

Alasdair MacIntyre (1999, 1) suggests this point in *Dependent Rational Animals*, where he seeks to come to terms with the strange fact that throughout the history of Western philosophy there are, "with some rare exceptions, only passing references to human vulnerability and affliction and to . . . our dependence on others." Instead, the normal condition of humanity is considered to be one of rational autonomy. Surprisingly (for an author not previously concerned with psychoanalytic theory), MacIntyre turns to Winnicott to argue that "acknowledgment of dependence is the key to independence" (85). Only when we recognize how much we truly need and depend on others can we find a place of freedom within networks of dependencies. Only then can we be dependent rational animals.

One should not give MacIntyre too much credit. He arrived late to his acknowledgment of dependence. Feminist theorists (I use the term broadly) such as Martha Nussbaum (1986), Jessica Benjamin (1988), and Jane Flax (1991), among many others, first taught us that the autonomous rational individual is itself a male fantasy, one to which women are not as predisposed. Why feminists have been more perceptive is not entirely clear. One imagines that it has something to do with women's traditional role of caring for the young and old, but fortunately answering the "why" question is unnecessary. Necessary is only to recognize that the acknowledgment of human dependency throughout the life cycle turns on its head much traditional political and social theory, making it much more difficult to equate freedom with autonomy and will.[3] (This is discussed in greater detail in chapter 4.)

Seen in this way, "freedom with" contains (and must contain) an element of sadness, of mourning for the loss of an absolute—the ideal of total freedom. If man or woman was totally free, he or she could not stand it. A number of informants, including those who expressed quite borderline visions of freedom, understood this point perfectly. As John put it, "I wouldn't want to be completely free. I don't think I could handle the burden of choosing for myself every second of the day." About this aspect of freedom, freedom as loss and limits, it may be that a borderline perspective is actually more helpful in drawing out the costs of absolute freedom for there is nothing limiting these losses. In any case, there is no reason to think that a troublesome view of freedom, freedom as a borderline experience, could not lead to insight by virtue of the extreme terms in which it formulates the problem, much as a caricature sometimes tells the truth about a person better than a portrait.

"Freedom with" understands that the thrill of transgression cannot be maintained; the exhilaration of breaking boundaries is by its nature limited. To live in freedom, as opposed to experiencing moments of freedom, is to abandon dreams of omnipotence and transcendence, dreams that generally have the quality of losing and fusing, both of which are experiences of the loss of boundaries. To live in freedom is to accept both limits and loss.

Consider a ballet dancer leaping across the stage, surely an icon of freedom. Without the rules and constraints of ballet, this freedom would be meaningless. Only by internalizing these rules and constraints can the dancer be free. This act of internalization is not one of grounding freedom; nor is internalization an act of false-consciousness, though it may be. Internalizing the rules of performance is, as Isaiah Berlin (1969, 141) points out, different from internalizing an ideology. We shall want to consider the nature of the frames and forms of freedom, paying attention to the irony of it all: only constraint makes freedom possible, which means there is a terrible danger of confusing the two, worshipping constraint as though it were freedom. The other danger is to imagine that freedom is the absence of constraint.

The image of freedom as "no limits and no boundaries" is not an image of freedom, but of narcissism, albeit an image that advertisers love to identify with freedom. "No boundaries" is also the slogan of the Ford Expedition sports utility vehicle.

In response to the image of the ballet dancer, one might pose the image of a child frolicking in a meadow. Certainly that requires no years of training, though it likely requires years of fortunate upbringing. Aren't some experiences of freedom just free? No. The child is bound by a thousand threads, made of gravity and of the nature of the experience of liberation itself, which is transitory. She cannot frolic forever, and after even a short while she will grow tired. If an overeager parent keeps egging her on, she will soon lose the pleasure in her frolic, and soon enough the freedom too. Freedom is a particular relationship to the rules and limits that frame and form, and in this way constitute (which is not the same as ground), the conditions of the experience of freedom. To understand freedom is to understand the quality of the relationship between the experience of freedom and its container, its limits.

The term "container" refers to everything that holds and sustains us, from friends and family to communities, constitutions, and institutions.[4] When they hold us lightly, these containers are the frames and forms of freedom. When these containers drop or crush us, then they endanger our freedom. These are, of course, abstract images, a way of trying to think about freedom that distinguishes between the experience and its enabling conditions, and so talk about freedom in a more nuanced way than all or nothing, no boundaries or imprisonment. In chapter 7, I argue that the Constitution of the United States is a pretty good container, neither crushing nor dropping its citizens.

"Freedom with" is not the whole of freedom. It is not, for example, a particularly good way of thinking about political freedom. Politics really *is* about the mastery of some over others. To ignore this via some misty-eyed vision of "freedom with" would be the worst false-consciousness of all.

We All Live between
Losing and Fusing

The terms "losing" and "fusing" refer not just to the poles of borderline experience, but to the poles of human experience: the threat of losing everything one values on the one hand, the threat of fusing with all that one values, and so losing oneself, on the other. We all live between losing and fusing, agoraphobia and claustrophobia. It is somewhere between these poles that freedom is experienced, though that puts it too spatially. Freedom is a way of negotiating and living with the dangers of agoraphobia and claustrophobia. In borderline experience, we see the poles more clearly only because we confront a way of being that lacks what it takes to modulate the swings between them: the cultivation of illusion.

No more than a couple of people who seemed borderline in the clinical, diagnostic sense were interviewed. Nor was there much connection between how split a person's experience of freedom was and how split the person's life was, though this was hard to tell in a one-hour interview. In other words, people whose accounts of freedom were severely split seemed no more likely to be living chaotic lives associated with borderline personality disorder. As a characterization of people's way of thinking about freedom, borderline is not a stalking horse for a psychiatric diagnosis.

One might argue that this weakens my argument. If borderline thinking about freedom is a psychological reality, then those who seem most borderline in clinical terms should think about freedom in the most borderline terms. I argue that the lack of correspondence strengthens my argument. Because individuals who don't seem borderline in the clinical sense talk about freedom in borderline terms means that this way of thinking about freedom is a real episode in the culture affecting us all. To be sure, only individuals can have borderline experiences; culture is an abstraction, a way of talking about the intellectual (in the widest sense) artifacts created by the men and women who make the culture. But, as Marx (2002) reminds us, while men and women make history, they do not make it with will or consciousness, and soon history turns around to make us. This is what is happening, especially among young people. Why it is happening is a topic to which I will turn shortly.

What then is the relationship between a culture of the borderline and a borderline personality? In arguing that there seems to be no connection between the clinical and cultural expressions of the borderline experience of freedom, don't I, in effect, put all the weight on the cultural expression of borderline experience? It's not so simple.

Something about the experience of freedom itself, I have argued, lends itself to the extremes of borderline thinking. I have characterized this "something" in terms of the way freedom seems to evoke experiences of losing and fusing, experiences that in turn activate and exploit the borderline tendencies in us all, the human task of living between agoraphobia and claustrophobia. Fearing the loss of all we hold dear, we seek to fuse with all we value, ending up feeling trapped, having to fight not just those who would deprive us of our values but our own desires for fusion as relief from the loneliness of losing. This, in any case, is my hypothesis about the affinity of freedom for the borderlines. My concern is not the disorganized and chaotic life of the clinically borderline man or woman, but the way in which an experience that lends itself to borderline thinking in us all is exaggerated by aspects of the culture.

What these aspects are is a leading theme of the last part of this chapter, as well as the chapters that follow. While I hesitate to give away too much, the key is informants' fear that in the end force and fate rule the world. It is this fear that exaggerates borderline tendencies in us all, especially in younger informants.

I did, in fact, interview one informant who was mentally disturbed, and in his case the extreme helped to flesh out the norm. Aaron told me that he was plagued with manic depression, subject to terrible mood swings that medication mitigated but did not eliminate. For Aaron, freedom meant knowing his roots, where he came from, a concept he explained in terms of Alex Haley's novel and then television series with the same title, now over two decades old. Aaron sees freedom this way, he said, because he knows what it is to become manic, losing his rootedness in reality. "You might think being manic is a feeling of freedom," he said. "It's not; it's a horrible feeling of not being able to find the limits of my reality. Freedom means remembering where I came from, my hometown, my family. Sometimes I recite their names, just to keep me grounded."

Aaron knows something important about freedom, the way in which the experience of limitlessness is not liberating but terrifying. The result, as the spiritual philosopher Simone Weil (2001) argues in *The Need for Roots*, is that it becomes impossible to change oneself, for there is no tradition, no container, no frame and form, within and against which one can define oneself. Rootlessness and the absence of boundaries aren't freedom. On the contrary, they make freedom impossible—Weil arguing that the rootless just go on to uproot others, the only truth they know.

Weil (1909–1943) is an interesting character, and one hesitates to introduce her as an exponent of freedom. Philosopher, activist, and religious seeker, she likely hastened her own death from tuberculosis by refusing food and medical treatment out of sympathy with the people of Occupied France. Weil's life is hardly the best example of a non-borderline vision of freedom. On the contrary, Weil seems to have defined freedom as the "decreation" of the self in order to return to God, a view that has some similarities with Marcuse's view of freedom but is incompatible with the view of freedom as a transitional experience. (The transition from life to willed death is not the transition Winnicott or I have in mind!) Weil is, however, the only woman thinker to seriously influence Iris Murdoch, and it is from this perspective that I occasionally turn to Weil. Murdoch's view of freedom is the subject of chapter 5. Murdoch often finds deep insight in those who are possibly insane, and in this regard one might view Weil as a figure out of Murdoch's fiction, except that to put it this way does a disservice to a noble if troubled woman.

Even a brief encounter with Weil reminds one of how reassuring the humane steadiness of Isaiah Berlin can be. Recall Berlin's distinction between negative and positive freedom. Negative freedom is to be left alone to do what one wants. Positive freedom is to possess the means of self-realization, a dangerous doctrine that may encourage tyranny. Though Berlin does not think about it this way (for Berlin, negative freedom is simply good, though it is not all that is good), I suggest that negative and positive freedom reflect the poles of borderline experience, the poles of losing and fusing. Negative freedom risks becoming "leave me alone, don't touch me, don't restrict me in any way," and so losing not just the human connections that make life worthwhile but also the frame and form of freedom itself, what Aaron calls roots. Positive freedom risks becoming the fusion of my will with all that is powerful and good, be it my higher self, God, the Party, or a thousand anarchists. Needed is a concept of freedom that sees negative and positive freedom not as competing definitions but as the ends to which freedom may be pursued, and so lost. Freedom is neither a place nor a possession. It is a delicate balancing act.

Many People Have Lost the Balance

Aspects of borderline thinking mark many of the things people say about freedom.

Freedom is of no value unless it is total and complete. If my wife can't see a medical specialist, then I am not free. If I have to drive to the beach, then I'm not free. The value of partial freedom, limited freedom, more rather than less freedom is not readily appreciated.

Freedom is either inner or outer, but there is not much of a connection between them. Freedom in the world doesn't add to inner freedom, and inner freedom is unlikely to inspire acts of freedom.

Freedom is mastery and money, and freedom is sleep and respite. We use the same word for both sets of experiences, but they have little to do with each other, almost as though their both being characterized by the term "freedom" is homonymous.

Freedom is devalued in the name of power. Because freedom depends upon the cooperation of others, it cannot be truly valuable, for dependence is a sign of weakness and vulnerability.

More symbolic and abstract aspects of freedom, such as freedom of speech, press, and assembly are irrelevant or effete because they do not directly affect me and my freedom right now. This seems closely related to the inability, characteristic of borderline thinking, to use symbols and myths, and so imaginatively participate in a more abstract freedom. In fact, it is this inability that accounts for so many of the remarkable things young people say about freedom. What I cannot adequately answer is where this inability comes from. To say "from the culture," or some such, is of course no explanation at all, just a restatement of the problem.

Berlin's concerns about positive freedom seem positively archaic from this perspective. To believe that my freedom is enhanced when I participate in a group that is self-governing or in an ideology that is triumphant (common examples of positive freedom), expresses an imaginative identification with a symbolic entity absent in most of the people I spoke with. Whatever the defects of the borderline experience of freedom, and they are significant, they do not lend themselves to the imaginary creation of a realm in which my freedom joins that of others to constitute the true meaning of positive freedom. What we need to worry about is the isolation, alienation, and anomie associated with borderline freedom. Otherwise expressed, borderline freedom does not allow itself to be bamboozled by the siren song of positive freedom. Those who experience freedom in borderline terms are likely to remain isolated and resentful, pursuing power as the simulacrum of freedom. Could there be worse fates than being bamboozled?

Though most people I spoke with reduce freedom to power, they are not clandestine followers of Nietzsche. They do not, in other words, embrace the will-to-power, not even in its most popular and banal version, the idealization of the capitalist adventurer in the novels of Ayn Rand, such as *Atlas Shrugged*. Not the will-to-power, but just power, is what most seek. There is quite a difference.

For Nietzsche (1968, 170–172), the will-to-power is the feeling that one is teeming with life, a feeling of abundance: abundant energy, potency, and the like. Generally, this is achieved through a process of overcoming pain. In a sense, the will-to-power is the opposite of narcissism, seeking to expand rather than shrink one's world. Indeed, one might regard Nietzsche's will-to-power as an illusion, sustained by the individual's ability to make out of his or her everyday life an epic encounter with all that is weak and ugly in human nature. Seen as a creative illusion, the will-to-power is the opposite of borderline thinking. Or, as Nietzsche (1968, 175) has Zarathustra put it, "I want to hear the thought that dominates you, and not that you escaped from a yoke." I know of no finer expression of positive freedom than this.

Informants, on the other hand, regard power as tantamount to money, something to possess so they can get what they really want. This is neither the will-to-power nor narcissism, but something more benign and almost as troubling, as it too leads to a withdrawal from the common world. Perhaps the best analog in political theory to what most people practice (and it is far from perfect) is what the author of *Democracy in America*, Alexis de Tocqueville (2000, 482–485), called "individualism." Fascinated with the cultural consequences of democracy in postrevolutionary America, Tocqueville sharply distinguished the individualism he found here from the egoism he knew from France. Egoism is selfishness. Individualism is a withdrawal from public life into the realms of family and making a living. In the end, thought Tocqueville, both are equally damaging to democracy. As people abandon the public world for private pursuits, the vacuum is filled by the ambitious and the unscrupulous. To be sure, some informants hope to return to the larger world, but only after making enough money to be free there. One doubts that most will complete the trip.

Other borderline themes are present in informants' views of freedom. One is the equation of freedom with the ability to "cut out, leave, just walk out the door and not come back." The man who put it this way had just learned that his girlfriend was pregnant, but he was far from alone in experiencing freedom in these terms, as though the only alternative to overwhelming obligation (fusing) was losing everything he cared about.

Not every person I spoke with saw freedom in borderline terms. If they had, I don't believe I would have been able to characterize the majority's experience of freedom as borderline, a phenomenon that stands out only by contrast, as I have argued. One who provided this contrast was Abe, who goes to college in New York City, but spends his summer and winter breaks in Israel. In New York he feels unfree because he doesn't fit in, but in Israel he feels unfree because everyone is so much like him that there is no escape. "I feel most free when I'm in an airplane, over the ocean somewhere between New York and Israel."

This is not a borderline formulation of freedom but its opposite, the imaginary creation of a symbolic buffer and resting place between the poles of losing and fusing. To be sure, Abe still experiences freedom in terms of fusing and losing. The difference is that he can connect the extremes in his imagination. Another difference is that he can make the connection without my asking about it. Not because his experience of freedom is whole and one, for it is not, but because the connection between the two types of experience is what he seeks.

One who saw freedom in similar terms was Martia, who grew up in a tiny town in East Germany. She was 12 years old when the Berlin Wall fell. In her small town she still fits in, a type of security that she equates with freedom. At the same time, life there is too confining, so after a few weeks she must leave again for the West, where she feels liberated but lonely. "I can never get it right. Either I feel secure but confined at home, or free but lonely in the West. I think I feel most free sitting in the window seat of a jet, flying to New York, imagining my mother hugging me good-bye, knowing I can go back."

Neither Abe nor Martia has an easy time of it, struggling almost constantly with the extremes of losing and fusing. What makes their views non-borderline is the centrality of the struggle itself, the way they know that neither pole will liberate them, for their freedom lies somewhere in the middle. One hopes that someday they will be able to bring this middle down to earth.

Both Abe and Martia are in their mid-twenties, but they sound more like older people, whose conceptions of freedom are less borderline. The big mystery, of course, is why. Does the way people think about freedom develop as people grow older, or did older people have different founding experiences of freedom? Would they have talked differently about freedom when they were younger, or would they have sounded more similar to younger people today? Earlier, I suggested that maturation is not the entire explanation; young people have had different formative experiences of freedom, experiences that will last a lifetime. I will pursue this argument. Nevertheless, it is clear that some experiences of freedom are only available to those who have lived a few decades. Only maturation allows certain experiences of freedom, though it certainly does not guarantee them.

One view of freedom that requires maturation is freedom as revealed power, based on the experience of having made plans and seen them through. "I feel most free when I look back and see that some of my dreams came true, that my dreams were not wasted, that I was able to do some of what I set out to do with my life." Even though Lila equates freedom and power, it is not a borderline formulation, as revealed by the use of terms such as "some." Lila did not need to realize every dream and every plan in order to feel free.

Another who knew something about "freedom with" is Gregory, the young man who experienced the Chesapeake Bay Bridge as a bridge of hands holding him up, allowing him to feel free. To appreciate the richness of this experience, it is important to know something about the Bay Bridge. It's over three miles long, and a section of it is very high. Driving over it feels like flying, and makes acrophobics crazy. Every year people have to be driven off the bridge by a state trooper stationed there to rescue panicked drivers paralyzed with fear. To experience the bridge as both flight and the work of hands at the same time is a complex experience of "freedom with."

What differentiates older and younger people is not that older people are less materialistic about freedom, less likely to equate freedom with power or money. What differentiates older and younger people is some older people's belief that one might have enough, that some power was enough power, some money enough money. As one older person put it, "freedom is getting a pension." Said another, "I don't know what freedom is, but I know what the opposite is. It's being sick without health insurance. It's being number 27 in line at the emergency room." A pension is not a multimillion-dollar fortune; health insurance is not the same thing as being independently wealthy. They are merely enough. The category of "enough" is the opposite of borderline experience. Enough is neither nothing nor everything but somewhere in-between.

Several older people expressed disappointment in freedom or rather in their own capacity to enjoy freedom. Charles put it this way, "Over the years I've learned that I don't have what it takes to be really free. I lack the independence. I choose to do things with my family that I don't want to do because it's easier that way."

You mean because you don't want to get into fights, I asked?

"No. Because it feels less lonely than going off on my own."

Because he has regrets, because he does not imagine that he has no freedom at all, because he does not redefine freedom as liberation from the ties that bind, Charles's view of freedom is not borderline. Freedom for Charles is one good among several. He wishes he had more freedom, but understands that the limits to his freedom are mostly internal. He might have redefined freedom as family belonging, but he is too honest to do that, even as one suspects he is being too hard on himself, as though his motives weren't pure enough to be the motives of a free man.

This suggests an important point. Those whose view of freedom is not borderline are not simply free. Far from it. One can't live one's life in an airplane. Abe and Martia may be rendering a symbol of non-borderline freedom, the airplane as flying bridge connecting the poles of losing and fusing, in terms too concrete. The inability to invest in symbols of freedom is, I have argued, a mark of borderline thinking characteristic of many I talked with. (It is also possible that I have worked a little too hard transforming their experience into a symbol.) Those whose view of freedom is not borderline have not, somehow, found the balance. Like Abe and Martia, they too struggle with the poles of losing and fusing, knowing something about the attraction of each pole, trying—not always successfully—to live somewhere in between. The point is they struggle. That is likely the best most of us can do.

One should not overemphasize the distinction between younger and older people's views of freedom. The differences are subtle, and some young people are more subtle than some old people. Indeed, it is not so much the difference between what young and old people say as the subtlety of the old that is striking, which is why young people are easier to interview. Their views often have a harder edge, making them easier to classify. By contrast, consider Maxim, a retired government official who spends almost all day every day with his wife. "I like my freedom in small doses. When [my wife's] out shopping, I'm on my own recognizance. But I wish I'd developed more skills at being alone."

As a rule, the term "own recognizance" refers to the release of a suspect from jail without his having to post bail, usually because he is well established in the community. Maxim knows something about his own lack of freedom, the fact that his needs and fears have become his jailer. He can even put this knowledge into a type of everyday poetry, but that doesn't change things. His tone is not one of "ah, but that's life." His tone is one of regret over a life not lived more fully. Does one want to say that Maxim's knowledge liberates him from the confines of his inability (as he sees it) to live more freely? Does his ability to think perceptively about how difficult it is for him to live between losing and fusing mean that his is not a troubled experience of freedom but a mature one? I'm not sure it does, though it would probably be more accurate to say that even mature experiences of freedom may be troubled. Freedom is not easy to live with.

The Opposite of Stoicism

In chapter 1, I suggested that a version of Epicurean freedom best captures the second dimension of freedom—freedom as respite—to which many people refer. Here I argue that a view the opposite of Stoicism best captures informants' experience of freedom as mastery. More precisely put, most people feel pressured to adopt a view of freedom the opposite of Stoicism, lest they have no freedom at all.

Cultivating indifference to worldly experience, the ancient Stoic sage sought to become master of his own will, the only thing that is completely within the individual's control, or so the Stoic believed. The modern experience of freedom is the inversion of Stoic freedom, says the political philosopher Hannah Arendt (2000, 438–444). Rather than becoming indifferent to worldly experience in favor of mastering my own experience, I project my experience with myself into the world. Since I can often will what I want within myself, I conclude that unless I can do the same in the world, then I am not free. Since in my imagination my freedom is boundless, moderns are led to conclude that freedom means overcoming all limits to my will. If moderns can't do this, then they are not free. Is this what younger people do? Is this the source of their romantic materialism?

At first I thought so. Young people really believe that they, or at least some people, can do what they will. Because we live in a world with others, this means that some others will not be able to do what they will. For many people it's that simple. Lacking among both older and younger people is any sense that this conflict with others has as its counterpart a conflict, or even a relationship, within the self. Charles and Maxim are exceptional in this regard. Few others talked about a conflict between higher and lower selves, though several said they would be freer if they could be less inhibited. This does not mean that most people are deficient in imagination. It means that they don't trust their imaginations in the face of concrete social reality.

Consider Sandra, who is convinced that freedom is internal, what she calls an experience of "disassociation," in which she can remove herself from worldly constraint, even the ties that bind her to loved ones. Sandra would be a Stoic if she could. But she can't. Sandra knows that it will take money and power for her to feel free in her life. She wishes it didn't, that she could be worthy of her ideal of inner freedom, but she knows she's not. "I wish I could feel free in myself, without any of the things that money can buy, like a good house and car. But I know I can't. I'm just not strong enough."

Sandra is the average young person, more articulate than most about her conflict; but a number of people are aware of it. While equating freedom with money and power or devaluing freedom in terms of money and power, most young people evince some regret over their choice. Sandra is unusual only in blaming herself, her own weakness, as much as she does, as if she were strong and pure enough no one could touch her freedom.

This is not, however, where Sandra goes wrong. Where Sandra goes wrong, where so many young people go wrong, is imagining that freedom has much to do with autonomy in the first place, at least as they define autonomy: independence from the power and money of others. For this is how most people think about freedom: as the ability to resist the intrusions of others with more money and power. And not just power and money. Ronaldo and a number of others see their freedom as challenged by their need for other people, as though freedom meant not just financial but emotional autarky. One wants to say that younger people hold a view of freedom similar to that of Hobbes. In Hobbes's view, freedom in the state of nature is virtually meaningless, as there is no security in which to enjoy it.

In fact, Hobbes's view of the liberty of subjects, as he called it, is more subtle and complex. For Hobbes, freedom is the ability to do whatever one wants without being blocked by physical impediments. We give up our freedom when we move from a state of nature to civil society, but because we do so willingly (or at least act as if we do) we should not complain about being restrained by laws, even those laws we do not participate in making. To complain about these laws is like complaining that one is "restrained from hurting" oneself (Hobbes, 1991, section 9.9). Hobbes, in other words, presumes an imaginary identification of citizens with each other, which is lacking in most young people. In other words, Hobbes is a theorist of positive freedom, a point not always recognized.

The view of freedom that comes closest to that of young people is the ancient Greek view of freedom as *autokratôr*, the most commonly used term for freedom among the Greeks.[5] The term comes down to us as autocrat, one who rules alone. The difference is that for the ancient Greeks the term *autokratôr* generally (but not always) referred to the freedom of the polis, a city state with sufficient power to govern itself. "In Athens . . . freedom required power, because power is a condition of freedom, but power proved in fact unobtainable without ruling others" (Momigliano, 1979, 149). For most people I spoke with, each individual is or would be his or her own city state. "Freedom is being the CEO [Chief Executive Officer] of my own life," said Sally. She meant *autokratôr*.

For a few young people, the ideal of *autokratôr* extends to nature itself. Ronaldo sees his freedom challenged by the laws of time and space themselves, as he can't move from his apartment to the beach in an effortless instant. Barbara said that real freedom would be to "take a crap" anywhere she wanted, anytime she wanted. There is something about freedom that brings out regressive urges.

Plato adopts the term *autokratôr*, transforming it into a category of moral psychology, one that refers to the rule of the higher part of the self over the lower, so that one can be master of oneself, rather than slave to one's desires (*Republic*, 443d–444e). Young people almost never go on to make Plato's distinction. For younger informants, the self is not divided, just beleaguered. Self-rule, the literal meaning of *autokratôr*, has nothing to do with ruling over oneself, but over others. (The parallel with Arendt's discussion of the changing meaning of freedom from ancients to moderns is apparent: in both cases, self-mastery is transformed into would-be world-mastery.) Like the ancient polis, one must acquire enough power over others so as to maintain one's freedom. We in the United States live in a world of 300 million individual poleis, each seeking to be *autokratôr*, which can only mean to amass enough power not to be subject to another's will. That is all there is as far as public life is concerned, a life lived in constant competition with others, what the Greeks called agony. Is it any wonder many people long for hot baths and sleep?

Why do young people see freedom as becoming *autokratôr*? Because there is so little idealism left. Idealism requires illusion. Idealism *is* illusion, the medium of transitional experience, the opposite of borderline experience, more akin to "freedom with." In idealism, inner freedom invests and enriches the outer world while remaining relatively immune to the corruption and cynicism of everyday life. It is this that so many people find so difficult and so threatening, evidently fearing that should their illusions see the light of day they will be crushed by the weight of the world. Reality is not just more powerful than illusion; reality is capable of crushing any illusion.

In the idiom of the popular culture, people seek mastery and control because they feel their lives are out of control. Though some young people spoke in these terms, mostly of being terribly busy, it was not my impression that they lived horribly chaotic lives. It was not even my impression that they believe they do. The quest for mastery and control comes from somewhere else. From where one can only speculate, based upon hours of listening to young people talk not just about their lives but their fears and values.

The best way to speculate is to quote the cleric Carel, in *The Time of the Angels*, a novel by Iris Murdoch (1966). Rector of a nonexistent church (it was bombed during the Second World War), Carel, who rarely leaves the rectory, seems to believe in angels, but not God. His daughter, his bishop, and others wonder if he is insane, but as in so many of Murdoch's novels it is the protagonist of doubtful sanity who has the deepest and most disturbing insight. This is Carel's.

Suppose the truth were awful, suppose it was just a black pit, or like birds huddled in the dust in a dark cupboard . . . [Suppose] there is only power and the marvel of power, there is only chance and the terror of chance. (171–172)

In their heart of hearts, many young people believe that the truth is just this awful. Not only do they have no idealism left, not only are they cynical, but they fear the worst is true, which is why they are in thrall to power and eager to amass as much as they can. Some know it won't help very much in the end, but there's no other game in town. "Let's say I got cancer. All the money in the world wouldn't help. I'd get a nicer room to die in, that's about it. But I'd still rather have the money."

One might be tempted to conclude that young people are greedy and selfish. As a general rule, this is not the case. Rather, they live unsheltered by illusion in the "empire of might," as Murdoch's tutor Simone Weil calls it, in which the only currency is power, master or slave the only roles available to any of us. "Only he who knows the empire of might and knows how not to respect it is capable of love and justice," says Weil (1977a, 181). Young people do not know how not to respect might, because almost nothing in their culture provides any guidance.

A Pharisee, continues Weil (1977b, 395), is someone who is virtuous out of obedience to the Great Beast of collective might, the might of public opinion. Young people aren't Pharisees either, and that is their great gift. They claim not virtue, but only necessity. Would that young people respected not necessity less but freedom more. For in the end most know that seeking mastery is not the path to freedom. They simply cannot imagine any alternative to mastery but slavery—that is, unfreedom. This is why Michael is stuck between being a suit or a bum, as he puts it.

It might seem simplistic to imagine a life of relaxation as an alternative to the pursuit of mastery, power, and money. Relaxation sounds like retirement, the same retirement that Alcibiades sought in the arms of the mistress of his dreams. Referring to a leading image of relaxation among the ancient Greeks (as well as among a number of informants), Weil says, "nearly all of the *Iliad* takes place far from hot baths. Nearly all of human life has always passed far from hot baths" (1977a, 155). Probably most of human life will always take place far from hot baths. Still, the *Iliad* is a poem of war, an activity in which the distance between the struggle for excellence, or survival, and hot baths is at its utmost. Isn't the goal of civilization to lessen that distance just a little?

A relaxed life expresses a profound and important vision of freedom. Of course, this requires that we understand the illusory nature of relaxation—that is, the way freedom depends upon illusion. One mark of the truths of Carel's dark cupboard is that not only are these truths utterly without illusion but they are incompatible with any illusion. This means they may be incompatible with freedom.

What remains are young people too honest to say that they have freedom when they don't believe it, but too cynical to imagine the freedom they might have. In other words, young people are immune to the illusions of freedom. That's good, in so far as young people are less likely to lie to themselves about freedoms they don't possess. That's bad if freedom is, by its nature, a type of illusion, the illusion of transitional experience to which Winnicott refers, an illusion that allows one to experience reality as filled with possibilities, even if the experience is as fleeting as "in the groove." If this is so, then most young people will never be free. They are much too realistic for that.

CHAPTER 3
BAD FAITH?

For many of a certain age, and not just professional intellectuals, Jean-Paul Sartre will always be *the* theorist of freedom, the one who made freedom not just a political slogan but also a personal project. One might imagine that given their individualistic understanding of freedom, young people would be taken with Sartre. Unfortunately, Sartre now belongs to the ages, or at least to another age. Few young people could say much about his philosophy.

One might respond that their ignorance hardly matters. Young people could be followers of (or fellow travelers with) Sartre without knowing it. Intellectuals love to label positions with the names of their leading exponents, and there is no reason to assume that every thoughtful person would know what the intellectual shorthand, "Sartre's view of freedom," stands for.

Sartre's view of freedom is that in our minds and imaginations, men and women are absolutely free. While we cannot make the world in any way that we want, we are free to interpret our world in any way we choose. The trouble is, I'm not the only one in the world. When I live with others, they become the enemy of my freedom, as it is everyone's natural tendency to see themselves through the eyes of others. In seeing myself this way, I betray my original freedom, defining my situation (indeed, my very being) in relationship to you. Nevertheless, in principle, I remain absolutely free, as I am free to give my life any meaning I choose. I am free to do this because I am not caused like a machine. My thoughts are beyond the realm of causation, though one might just as well say that my thoughts are self-caused.

Among Sartre's most famous concepts, or perhaps I should simply call it an epithet, is bad faith (*mauvaise foi*). Bad faith refers to the way people escape the freedom they already have by denying that they have it. For Sartre, freedom has nothing to do with the fact that the world resists my will. Freedom means I have a choice as to how to react about everything that happens to me, and how to come to terms with it. Indeed, Sartre holds that for the most part we choose our passions, such as whether to be angry or depressed. Somewhere deep inside each one of us there is an empty space, what Sartre calls *Néant*, or nothingness, which no one and no thing can touch. That place is freedom, for in it I can give the events of my life any meaning I choose. For example, I might see prison as a chance to liberate myself from a life of crime.

Ignorant of the "coefficient of adversity of the given," as Sartre calls it, young people believe that the resistance of the world to their wishes means they are unfree (Sartre, 1956, 628). On the contrary, this resistance is the stage on which a person's freedom is made meaningful. It is only because the world resists that young people (indeed anybody) have a chance to be free: absent the resistance of the world, freedom would be absolutely pure and completely meaningless, the liberation of angels. Freedom would be meaningless because there would be nothing to be free from or to. Even dancing involves the resistance of the world: gravity, the forms and traditions of the dance, and so forth. It is likely that Sartre would not, in other words, secretly admire younger informants as I do. Sartre would, however, recognize in the answers of the young people many of the themes of his life's work.

In his earlier and better-known work, *Being and Nothingness*, Sartre held that the other person is always the enemy of my freedom, the sinkhole of my consciousness. "The other is the hidden death of my possibilities . . . In the jolt that I feel when apprehended by the Other's look, suddenly I experience a subtle alienation of all my possibilities" (1956, 354). Hell is other people, because once I encounter another person, I cannot help but think about myself and my plans in terms of how the other sees me. Even if I oppose the other in every way I can, I am still defining myself in terms of the other. From this hell there is No Exit, the title of Sartre's most famous play. Hell is other people because they refuse to mirror and confirm me, as I refuse to mirror and confirm them. If I did, I would be their slave. In Sartre's world, everyone wants to be free, and no one wants to be a slave, with the result that none are free.

It would be misleading to say that the young people I spoke with feel trapped in a world with other people. Rather, they feel trapped by the sheer contingency of the social world, in which they are not rich and not powerful. Because they know it could as easily be otherwise, they feel resentful and imprisoned. This is as close as they come to Sartre's nausea. It's closer than one might suppose.

For Sartre, nausea is an experience of the sheer, brute facticity of the world. Not only is the world not my idea, not only does the world not care about me, but the world is simply there—brute, real, and thing-like.

The result is a loss of boundaries, as the sheer mass of the world begins to melt together, sucking me in. *Nausea* is the title of Sartre's (1938) earliest novel, the story of Antoine Roquentin, a writer who is horrified at his own existence, with the fact that he merely exists, that he just is. It isn't necessary that he exist; he might not have existed at all, and one day he won't. There is no Idea that makes his existence necessary. He just is.

The novel's most famous scene reads like it came from a Stephen King horror story. Sitting on a bench in the park beside a chestnut tree, Roquentin begins to feel that the roots of the tree are monstrous, naked in their mere being there, somehow about to absorb him. "I would," he writes in his diary, "have liked them to exist less strongly, more dryly, in a more abstract way, with more reserve. The chestnut tree pressed itself against my eyes" (1964, 127). Like the stereotypical academic, Roquentin wants the chestnut tree to be subject to his Idea of the tree. That's what makes Roquentin's life absurd: life's sheer contingency, that it just is, and so is he.

Informants are not younger versions of Roquentin. None seemed horrified by the mere existence of the natural world, though perhaps the progress of science and technology since 1938 has had a hand in this, as though humans might some day no longer be subject to nature's contingency. Not nature, but the contingency of the social world is what horrifies young people, particularly the way in which the distribution of wealth and opportunity, and with it freedom, seem so utterly arbitrary. Sean put it this way. "It's disgusting. All these powerful people can do anything they want, and I can't even take a vacation. Sometimes I feel sick when I think of all the things I can't do."

Similar to the experience of nausea is the way the unequal distribution of power is experienced as contingent, so utterly meaningless that it threatens all meaning. This is the defining characteristic of nausea, as things become separated from their names. Nothing means anything except that it is a thing (Sartre, 1964, 125). "They have power and I don't, but it could just as easily have been the other way around," said Jane. "It's just a matter of luck." Power compels but at the same time power is meaningless, because who's got it seems arbitrary.

Simone Weil (1977c, 457) makes a similar point. It is not just might that causes us to suffer, but the caprice of might, the way it might not have been but is, that causes affliction. With the term "affliction" (*malheur*), Weil means not just pain and suffering, but the loss of the meaning of life. This is what makes some young people sick: that the truth is as awful as Carel the mad cleric imagines, a dark cupboard filled with nothing but power and fate. Only, for some young people it is not a dark cupboard but a simple reality anyone can see by the light of day.

What we really want, says Sartre, is to be pure potential (being-for-itself) and realized facticity (being-in-itself) at the same time. The desire to be God, Sartre (1956, 724) calls it. What we want is for our potential to remain infinite, which must mean, of course, that it is never realized. Only God is infinite potential and realized actuality at the same time. For the rest of us, once we put our potential into practice, it is no longer infinite. Even if I become the best baseball player who ever lived, I will never be as good as I might imagine in my wildest dreams.

A simple example from my own experience might help to explain. When my grandson was younger, he wanted to go to the store with his mother. At the same time, he wanted to stay home and play a game with his older brother. "You have to choose," we said. "You can do one or the other, but not both."

"But I want to do both!" he cried.

We got smart, or so we thought. "First you can go to the store with your mother, and when you come back and we finish dinner then you can continue the game with your brother."

"I don't want to do one and then the other," sobbed my grandson. "I want to do both at once."

Alternatives exclude, which means that we will always be less than perfectly free. It took my grandson several more years to accept this, and I'm not sure he ever really has. I'm not sure anyone really does, which is likely why so many people said they feel most free when they are asleep. In sleep, illusion and reality are one. External reality is suppressed and alternatives need no longer exclude. As Sigmund Freud (1959, 80) puts it,

> by being born we have made the step from an absolutely self-sufficient narcissism to the perception of a changing external world and the beginnings of the discovery of objects. And with this is associated the fact that we cannot endure the new state of things for long, that we periodically revert from it, in our sleep, to our former condition of absence of stimulation and avoidance of objects.

In one way or another, many of the young people, and of course Sartre, are equating an absolutely self-sufficient narcissism with freedom. The difference, of course, is that Sartre figured out that this wish was not to be. The moment we insert our imagination into the world, we become unfree. Many young people are not yet quite convinced of this. In this adheres their radicalism.

Sartre says that the skier doesn't just want to glide freely down the slope. He wants to "*possess* this field of snow," to own the mountain (1956, 743, his emphasis). It is not enough to move freely through the world. One must possess it, dominate it, and make it one's own. By this Sartre means that the skier transforms the meaning of the snow, so that it becomes a vehicle for his ambitions. One cannot, in this view, be free unless and until one finds oneself at home in the world, and one does this only by discovering that one has made it one's own. Unless one can do this, one must live in the slime of contingency forever. There are but two choices: to possess the world or to be possessed by it, what Sartre calls nausea.

No young people talked in quite these terms, but Lloyd came close, closer perhaps than Sartre imagined.

"Do you know why I study so hard, why I make such good grades?" he asked. "Because society is heading downhill. Socially, economically, every way, we are headed for an avalanche. I study hard so that I will be successful, so that there will be as many bodies as possible between me and the bottom when it all comes crashing down."[1]

Sartre's images are often complicated. For Sartre (1956, 743–747), skiing on the snow represents a relationship of sliding over the surface so as not to be possessed by the object. One skis to avoid taking root. Snow is the opposite of the slime of nausea, the way things stick to one. Skiing also represents the possession of the virginal and pure. For Lloyd, the bodies of others are not to be skimmed over; they are big, dumb cushions of flesh, and in that sense at least they have a slimy quality.

Lloyd has grasped the implication of the reduction of freedom to power. The reduction means that I do not wish to be free in a world of others who are similarly free, an ideal of Sartre's later work. Rather, I wish to dominate and possess others as the only alternative to being dominated and possessed. Here is my closest approach to an important aspect of borderline experience that I have until now neglected—rage. Almost all who theorize about borderline states make rage central, even as they differ on its sources. For example, is rage an expression of an unconscious desire to fuse with the unavailable person or object, as Kernberg suggests (Kernberg, 1995, 68)? Yet, rage was not an experience central to my interviews. Few informants expressed anything that came close to rage, either in tone and feeling, or in content. Perhaps this had to do with the fact that mine was one interview, not a protracted analysis. Probably it had as much or more to do with the fact that I was not interviewing men and women with a borderline personality disorder but men and women who live in a culture with a borderline conception of freedom. In this cultural dimension, not rage but fear of being unable to resist the forces that held Carel in awe, the forces of fate and might, is the leading passion. One can see how this passion might readily turn to rage, but among those I interviewed it more often was experienced as bafflement turned to cynicism.

Of all informants, Lloyd probably came closest to the classical construction of borderline rage, expressed in his utter disregard for the integrity of others, his refusal to accept Kant's equation of ethics with a single dictum: treat others as ends not means. If we see rage not merely as the overt expression of hatred but as a cynicism so complete that its possessor would treat fellow humans as things, seeing that as the only recipe for survival, then perhaps the cynicism of the borderline experience of freedom *is* rage. Certainly this is the ethical danger many informants face, the tendency to become so deeply cynical about the absence of justice in a world in which force and fate rule that they join with rather than resist this reality. This too is a type of fusion.

Many young people talk about power as a means of securing a type of free space around themselves into which others cannot intrude, and within which they have all they need. In this sense they do not want to possess the world. They do, however, want to own a piece of it. As Sandra put it, "I don't need to own land, or even a house. I just need to have lots of money. That way I don't have to be a slave to my boss, or depend on anybody else." Sandra does not want to possess the snow. She wants to possess her freedom as though it were an expensive commodity. Sartre would remind her that she already has it gratis.

To be sure, no one even came close to saying hell is other people. Yet, the idea that the other is the enemy of my freedom is a leading theme. Consider the story told by Ally.

"The most free I ever felt was on a vacation to Colorado. We [Ally, her parents, and some friends] went riding on this huge mesa, and I got lost on purpose. Just me and my horse. I thought I'd be scared but I wasn't. I was free, riding with the wind. Until I heard my sister calling for me. She broke into my dream, and I couldn't get her to leave."

This story could be misleading were it taken to suggest that what connects the young people with Sartre is being intruded upon in the midst of experiences of total involvement in the world, much as Jean Genet was intruded upon by the gaze of one who labeled him a thief (Sartre, 1963). No, what connects Ally with the Sartre of *Being and Nothingness* is the sense that others, even friends and lovers, are only hostile to her freedom. Others may provide love and comfort. Ally knows she needs her family. But they can contribute nothing to her freedom. Freedom is being untouchable, or at least untouched. Like most young people, she does not imagine that freedom might be a shared achievement, "freedom with."

Recall the "panic state" that Ronaldo fell into when he realized that perfect freedom meant perfect isolation. Or consider the puzzled Clara, who says, "Freedom is my birthright. I get it just for being me . . . But that doesn't make sense either. How can someone take away my freedom if I'm born with it? Then it's more like a driver's license. They can take it back."

Because one is free inside one's self, one concludes the world must correspond to this state of being or one is not free. Stoicism in reverse seems the best label for this assumption. For some people, this assumption is unacceptable and so they remain stuck and puzzled, like Ronaldo and Clara. Others simply draw the obvious conclusion. "I'm not going to say I'm free if I'm not," said Tom in exasperation. I'd been gently (I thought) challenging his claim that he was unfree. "I don't have to be free to have a decent job, family, kids, the things people say they want. I'm just not going to lie about it and call it freedom."

One might argue that Stoicism in reverse applies not just to young people but also to Sartre. Or rather, young people and Sartre conclude much the same thing. Who was more brilliant than Sartre in characterizing the permutations by which the absolute freedom of consciousness is irretrievably lost once it enters the world? The difference is that Sartre made a distinction between the facts of experience and the meaning of experience. This distinction comes closer to the old Stoicism than the new.

The term "old Stoicism" refers to Stoic philosophers such as Epictetus, who says, "What upsets people is not things themselves but their judgments about the things" (*Handbook*, 5). The "new Stoicism" refers to the "Stoicism" (really Stoicism in reverse) that makes no distinction between meaning and fact. Not "what upsets people is their judgment about things," but "what upsets people is that their will is not powerful enough to overcome the resistance of the world" is the motto of the new Stoicism.[2]

The old Stoicism requires an inner world, a space of illusion, akin to what Sartre calls *Néant*, a space of negation in which conventional meaning can be given an unconventional twist. It is this space that seems to be missing in many young people. Why it is missing is the focus of chapter 4 on Marcuse, though I have already suggested the reason in chapter 2. Illusion, the transitional space between being and nonbeing, is the first thing to go in borderline thinking, as the world is divided into losing and fusing. *Néant* is a space of illusion.

One wants to say that throughout all the twists and turns of Sartre's project, he remained steadfast in his view that human freedom is the freedom to give the facts of experience the meaning we choose. What changes in Sartre's later works is the nature of the "we," so that by the time of the *Critique of Dialectical Reason* (2003), meaning-giving is a collective human practice. Others can help us negate an oppressive reality.[3] Although one wants to say this, it is not so simple. In his last book, Sartre held that due to the burden of his childhood, Gustav Flaubert was simply incapable of seeing himself as agent or actor in the world (Sartre, 1981). Flaubert had no choice about that. But, if Flaubert was incapable of transforming the self that was made of him, he retained a modicum of freedom, a tiny space between what was made of him and what he eventually became. In this space—a much reduced but still potent *Néant*—freedom is located. In a late interview, Sartre says,

> I believe that a man can always make something of what has been made of him, that is the definition I would give today of freedom, the little movement which makes of a totally conditioned social being a person who does not reproduce in its entirety what he received from his conditioning. (Sartre, 1974, 35)

It is in this tiny space that freedom continues to be located.

The young people I talked with don't think in these terms. They are not overtly troubled by the possibility that their values and choices may be purely conventional, and in this sense inauthentic. One reason is ironic detachment. They are not fully invested in their roles. In some respects this is good. Sartre (1956, 101–102) famously mocks a waiter for being so invested in the role of waiter that he becomes a clockwork man. The young people interviewed are not likely to do that. "I'm not who I appear to be," said Peter, with a sly smile. He meant that he would not always be, and did not consider it in his nature to be, the student and bartender he is right now. He hopes to be rich and powerful one day. He will trade a less desirable conventional role for a more desirable one.

Peter is a thoughtful young man, and one suspects that he will not be fully invested in the more desirable social role either, should he achieve it. But he will not be holding himself back in order to participate in richer, more imaginative, less conventional roles. His equation of freedom and power will see to that. Like most younger informants, Peter does not imagine freedom as a gap or space between actual and potential. For most young people, freedom is actual or it does not exist. This is both their charm and their downfall. For example, few young people talked of freedom in terms of richly personal hopes and dreams. Surely some young people chose not to share the rich and diverse content of their dreams. On the other hand, it was not my impression that most people were withholding. On the contrary, they shared much about their personal lives that surprised me, such as stories of unwanted pregnancy, betrayal, and drug use. An hour is a long interview, and the questions were open-ended. Had most young people been more imaginative about the content of freedom, I think I would have noticed.

For most people, freedom is the power to do what one wants, the content of which is largely conventional. Freedom is, in other words, so concrete that it lacks the quality of a space of negation. To stand back from one's role in the absence of this space is not creating new possibilities for negation. It is just standing back, what is called ironic detachment, the leading mode of being in the culture of narcissism, as Christopher Lasch (1979) reminds us.

Conventionalists or Radicals?

Certainly most young people view the content of their freedom in strictly conventional terms. But there is nothing conventional about the way in which most young people want to possess their freedom, as though their freedom must be limitless in order to be real. "Limitless" not in the sense of there can or should be no limits to their power and will. Young people don't think like this. But limitless in the sense of their tendency to define freedom as material, concrete, real, and now, in every aspect of my life, or it does not exist and hence means nothing. Ronaldo is exemplary. His liberty to go to the beach almost every afternoon in the summer is not real freedom because he has to drive in traffic following the rules of the road in order to get there.

Does this make the young people narcissists? Yes, but they don't act like narcissists. They act like solid citizens on the make. Their narcissism is confined to their dreams, or rather to a concept of limitless freedom that resides in lives and minds defined by limits. One could conclude that the young people are conventionalists and narcissists at the same time, narcissistic conventionalists or conventional narcissists. Closer to the truth, this way of putting it would still overlook how radical their claim to freedom truly is.

Imagine thinking that the term "freedom" must mean something real and concrete, or it means nothing. If my boss can order me around at work, then I'm not free. If my wife can't see a medical specialist, then she (and we, an interesting and encouraging variation) is not free. If I have to sit in traffic for two hours every day, then I'm not free. To even imagine that freedom ought to liberate me from the mundane constraints of everyday life is radical, even (or especially) if most young people conclude that they likely will never be free. For many this is acceptable. Life remains worth living and is often satisfying. It's just not free.

Like Tom, the young man who refused to say he was free when he didn't believe it, most young people were not deeply depressed about not being free. They just weren't going to lie about it. Robert put it a little differently. "Freedom isn't everything. A person who's doing what he wants to do doesn't need additional freedom." Robert's view sounds so similar to Tom's, and yet there is a subtle difference. Tom remains resentful about his lack of freedom, even (or especially) in the midst of a fairly comfortable and satisfying life. Robert, who's retired, seems content not to question whether he is free or not, as long as he's living the life he wants. He is, in other words, allowing freedom to possess the quality of an illusion, something that we do not have so much as participate in, even—or especially—when we don't keep asking whether we have it.

That I have interpreted Tom's view of freedom correctly, a view that is widely shared, is supported by one independently wealthy young man I interviewed, a dot.com millionaire as they are called, who sold his share in a computer networking company for millions before the bubble burst. He said that he didn't believe his views on freedom would be very helpful to me because he didn't have to contend with the constraints of everyday life, such as getting up at a particular time, going to work, making a living, following a schedule, listening to the boss, or accepting second best in anything. In other words, he defined freedom much as other young people do. The difference is he had it. Whether it made him any happier is hard to tell.

For Sartre, freedom means responsibility. To be authentic means not just to accept my freedom but also my responsibility for all that I choose. If I choose to go to war, then I am responsible for the war (1956, 708; 1999, 41). Sartre's reason for equating responsibility and freedom changes during the course of his career, but central throughout is something like Nietzsche's concept of loving one's fate (*amor fati*). As Anthony Farr (1998, 86) puts it,

> the radical nature of "choice" in Sartre's thought corresponds with the *amor fati* in Nietzsche's work: it is the demand that we accept this world as ours, and do not attempt to waste time dividing every situation into what I intended and what is fate, misfortune or chance ... We must learn to acknowledge that the reality of the word, however hostile or obstructive it may be, belongs to us. Every situation mirrors my being.

"Ignominious adaptation" to one's prison is what Theodor Adorno, founder of the Frankfurt School of Critical Theory (1974, 97–98), calls *amor fati*, and he is just right. I must endure reality, perhaps I must accept it, but there is no reason reality must be loved. Who says every situation mirrors my being? Are my choices as powerful as all that? Is that too not a species of narcissism, one not shared by the young?

Young people don't equate freedom with responsibility.[4] This has its downside, as they often seem almost willfully ignorant of the freedoms they do possess—of mind, spirit, place, time, and even youth. Their failure to equate freedom and responsibility has its upside as well. Young people refuse to ignominiously adapt themselves to what many see as the prison of everyday life. Better to say one is not free than to claim freedom while stuck in a little cubicle at work all day. In some respects, young people are more honest than Sartre. In some respects they make Sartre sound like an apostle of the power of positive thinking.

If young people are more honest then Sartre in one respect, they have not been on his prodigious journey, and it seems unlikely that they will. At the heart of Sartre's journey is his realization that freedom is not just an act of individual authenticity but a collective practice. (What this collective practice might look like in today's world is the focus of chapters 6 and 7.) Throughout Sartre's work, freedom remains an expression of the translucidity of consciousness, a fancy way of saying that the mind may always know itself. There are no unconscious parts of myself permanently closed to insight and change. Deep down the coward knows that he has the freedom to be brave if he chooses. In his later works, beginning as early as the last pages of *Being and Nothingness*, Sartre (1956, 797–798) intimates a connection between my freedom and that of others. If freedom is a value, then it is valuable for all, so that my freedom is increased when yours is, as there is now more freedom in the world.

Young people don't see much of a connection between their freedom and that of others, unless it is simply negative or zero–sum, in the language of game theory so popular today: more freedom for you means less for me. This is, in the end, the weakness of young people's vision, which greatly resembles Thomas Hobbes's account of life in the state of nature as the war of all against all. In such a world, one strikes first in order not to be a victim.

If one imagines a civilized version of Hobbes's war of all against all, then one can imagine the world that many young people live in, a world in which my freedom depends upon how much power and money I can amass before others acquire them first. If this conclusion seems extreme, the reader should note that at least one political theorist has reached it first. "Modern politics is civil war carried on by other means, and *Bakke* [a 1978 Supreme Court decision outlawing quotas in medical school admissions] was an engagement whose antecedents were at Gettysburg and Shiloh" (MacIntyre, 1981, 236). In this world of constant conflict, freedom as respite is only available in small doses, generally late at night when the previous day's engagement is over and the next day's is not yet begun.

The trouble with this vision is that it neglects all the ways in which people might cooperate in order to secure and enhance their collective freedom. With the term "collective" I refer not to the freedom of the collective (whatever that might mean), but the freedom of a group of cooperative individuals, one by one. I say this not in the spirit of the Sartre (1999, 57–60), who wrote in "The Humanism of Existentialism" that I have an obligation to will the freedom of others, an obligation I can hardly avoid. If I think freedom is good, then it must be good for all. The Kantian side of Sartre was never his most convincing aspect. I say this as a political scientist who knows that right now relatively small groups of people are organizing to extend their power and influence over others. Young people who equate power with freedom, but who do not know or understand that both are in the end a social project, may end up with neither.

CHAPTER 4

MASTERY AND RESPITE

Radical students in the 1960s referred to them as the "3 M's": Marx, Mao, and Marcuse. Though there is nothing politically radical about most of the young people I talked with, their view of freedom is—in its own way—about as radical as that of Herbert Marcuse. Marcuse can help explain the strange split in their accounts between freedom as mastery and freedom as respite, showing why young people can hardly imagine a world in which these two dimensions of freedom might coexist a little more comfortably. In other words, Marcuse can help explain the borderline quality of many people's experience of freedom. He can't cure it but he can explain what it would take to do so.

One might respond that there is nothing radical about young people's views of freedom. Wanting to be *autokratôr* isn't radical, just narcissistic and demanding. In this regard, young people are about as radical as Emma Bovary. Perhaps, but it is good to recall how much Marcuse finds to admire in Madam Bovary, above all the way her almost crazed demand for happiness and satisfaction challenges bourgeois society. Most of the young people interviewed have their feet firmly planted on the ground. Nevertheless, their naïve belief that freedom means they should be able to do what they want deserves our awe, if not our respect. Why this belief has not translated itself into a more radical politics is among the concerns addressed by Marcuse.

If one were going to label Marcuse, the term cultural Marxist would come closest to the mark, suggesting someone who believes in the primacy of the material world, above all the world of labor, but nonetheless believes that aspects of culture live a life of their own. One might also call Marcuse a psychoanalytic Marxist, for no one before or since worked harder to marry Marx and Freud, an odd couple indeed: the man who made labor and revolution primary coupled with the man who made sex and repression his leading themes. Regardless of how one labels Marcuse, however, the problem Marcuse faced is the same problem all Western Marxists faced after the First World War. Who is going to lead the revolution now that the proletariat no longer cares about anything but wages, hours, and fringe benefits? Among those troubled by this problem was the Frankfurt School of Critical Theory. Founded in Germany in the years before the Second World War, its leading members included Max Horkheimer, Theodor Adorno, and of course Marcuse, who became the School's most famous member, at least in the United States, where all three found asylum during Hitler's reign, but where only Marcuse chose to remain.

Sometimes one has the impression that Marcuse (1969, 1972) looked too hard for a proxy for the proletariat, placing too much hope in the denizens of the counterculture of the 1960s and 1970s, who in hindsight seem to have been even more readily co-opted than the proletariat. Am I also looking too hard, trying to find some—any—revolutionary potential in the young people I interviewed? Certainly these young people are a peculiar group, falling somewhere between the proletariat, which has been absorbed into the middle class, and Madam Bovary, who wanted so much more.

The novel is no longer widely read, so it may help to recall its plot.[1] Miserable in her marriage to Charles, the decent but dull town doctor, the beautiful and bored Emma Bovary finds romance and temporary transcendence in a series of adulterous affairs. At the same time as she is carrying on with her lovers, Emma is piling up enormous debts to her clothier, who encourages her to indulge her every fancy as though she were the wealthy woman she imagines herself to be. Eventually the house she owns with her husband is sold off to pay her debts, and Emma is disgraced. Resolving to die a noble death, Emma swallows arsenic, which results not in a dignified death but a horrifying lingering demise. Broken by the knowledge of his wife's infidelity, Charles dies within the year, leaving a legacy of but 12 francs to support his orphan daughter. That's it.

Emma Bovary is deeply corrupted by her narcissism and envy. It was not my impression that most young people are comparably corrupted. On the contrary, they did not appear deeply envious of those richer and more powerful than themselves. Most are simply convinced that the rich and powerful are, by definition, more free. Not necessarily happier, just more free, because that's what freedom is. Freedom is real, and it's now, and it means I can do what I want. To hold to this view in the midst of a life governed by capricious bosses, impenetrable bureaucracies, and reified social systems is not just narcissism; it represents a dream of liberation in which Marcuse would find hope.

Had she lots of money, Emma Bovary's behavior would have been considered normal for her class, her affair hardly cause for scandal. Because she was not wealthy, her extravagance destroyed her. Young people are not as a rule self-destructive. As a group they seem remarkably down-to-earth. They have the viewpoint of Madam Bovary, a combination of narcissism and convention, in the body of a bourgeoisie. It's not the worst combination, particularly when one considers why Herbert Marcuse (1978) admires Madam Bovary—because she wants more, because she won't accept the lie that self-sacrifice is happiness, that work is satisfying, that constraint is freedom.

Utopia

Unlike Marx, Marcuse held that labor is inherently unfree, no matter how it is socially organized, no matter who owns the means of production, because in labor the thing itself, that which is labored upon, always comes first. Marcuse calls this the "Law of the Thing" (*Getsetz der Sache*). Never in labor but only in play can men and women be free. "In a player's single throw of a ball lies an infinitely greater triumph of human freedom over objectification than in the most enormous accomplishment of technical labor" (1965b, 14–15, my translation). In play, we play with ourselves and for ourselves. Only when we do that are we free. The people I talked with would understand.

One way to think about Marcuse's claim is to compare it with Sartre's vision of freedom. For Sartre, one is absolutely and completely free, but only in one's imagination, what he calls *Néant*. Once I begin to act, I encounter a world of others who care nothing about my freedom. Some of these others are things, such as Roquentin's chestnut tree, which simply and terrifyingly is. Some of these others are people, who generally have dreams of their own, which rarely if ever mirror mine. To act on my freedom is to limit it, but there is no other way, no alternative except perhaps to remain locked up in my own mind.

Occasionally, however, one encounters another human whose dreams mirror one's own. We call these others mothers or lovers, people who seem to see us as we want to be seen. Sartre points out how much conflict there is even between lovers, each struggling to get the other to see him or her as he or she wants to be seen. Though they are hardly lovers, the protagonists of Sartre's greatest play, *No Exit*, are locked in this conflict for all eternity. The macho hero who may have died a coward's death, the aging coquette, and the working-class lesbian: each will mirror the other for a moment before going on to smash the mirror, and with it a facet of the other's existence.

Marcuse, by contrast, imagines a world in which even nature comes to mirror my desires, so that the world itself comes to cooperate in sustaining the illusion that it has been playfully created by humans. This would be Winnicott's ideal of transitional experience extended to the scale of humanity's relationship to the planet, nature as the ultimate transitional object, complement of my desires. Was there ever a greater utopian than Marcuse, who characterizes his ideal in terms of the Nirvana principle?

> The redemption of pleasure, the halt of time, the absorption of death: silence, sleep, night, paradise—the Nirvana principle not as death but as life. Baudelaire gives the image of such a world in two lines:
>
> > There all is order and beauty,
> > Luxury, calm, and sensuousness
>
> This is perhaps the only context in which the word *order* loses its repressive connotation: here, it is the order of gratification which the free Eros creates. (1966, 164)

Socialist revolution will not bring paradise in its train. Labor must not just be transformed but eliminated. This, Marcuse believes, has finally become possible, at least in the foreseeable future. Scientific and technological progress, coupled with socialist revolution, might make it possible that men and women would no longer need to labor. The alienation of labor would be complete, by which Marcuse means that no longer would the world be divided into the realms of necessity (labor) and freedom (play). Necessity and freedom would finally coincide in the realm of freedom. Virtually all repression, including psychological repression, would become "surplus," as men and women discover that it is not the nature of civilization but the nature of repressive civilization that requires men and women to suppress their desires in order to labor.

Joining Marx and Freud as no one before or since, Marcuse argues that the abolition of labor would allow the transformation of the psyche itself. Psychological repression would be unnecessary. Machines would do the real labor, and the tasks that remained would be undertaken in the spirit of creative play.

Marcuse writes in the utopian tradition of Francis Bacon, for whom science, technology, and industry will change everything, including—in Marcuse's case—not just human nature but world nature. No longer at war with their own repressed desires, men and women could approach each other and the world in the spirit of play and Eros. Human Eros will find its complement in the Eros of nature. "Such a world could (in a literal sense!) embody, incorporate, the human faculties and desires to such an extent that they appear as part of the objective determinism of nature" (Marcuse, 1969, 31).

If freedom is an illusion in Winnicott's sense—that is, an agreement not to ask whether the other is created by me or merely other—then Marcuse would draw nature itself into this illusion in order to make men and women free. Sartre, on the other hand, ends the process prematurely. Sartre, says Marcuse, "revives Hegel's formula for the free and rational condition of man." Hegel implies that one day history and reason will coincide; the way things are will finally be the way they should be. Sartre, on the other hand, "takes the ontological shortcut and transforms the process into the metaphysical condition of the 'pour-soi' [for-itself]" (1973, 175).

With the odd phrase "ontological short cut," Marcuse means that Sartre assumes that humanity's current situation, epitomized by the objectivity of the chestnut tree, reflects the nature of objectivity itself, the way the world just is, so massive, other, and real. About this, suggests Marcuse, Sartre is mistaken. Approached with the proper attitude, the world itself might yet turn another more benign aspect to humanity.

What this proper attitude looks like—that is, how we might get from here to there, from a world that cares nothing for the human being, to a world that mirrors human freedom, is not spelled out by Marcuse. Does E. F. Schumacher (1999) or Charles Fourier (1971) come closer to the mark? Marcuse does not say. What is clear is that we shall have new culture heroes. Neither the wily Odysseus nor the noble Prometheus, who struggles against his own pain to create civilization, but Orpheus and Narcissus shall be our new champions. Orpheus represents the voice that does not command but sings, while Narcissus gives himself over to the call of silence, sleep, night, and even death.

Marcuse's vision is totally utopian and absolutely ridiculous, right? Probably. Not only is Marcuse's utopia impossible it is also regressive, idealizing as its culture two heroes who spurn genuine human relatedness in almost all its forms. Let us not forget what happens to these two antiheroes. Orpheus is torn to pieces by enraged maidens whom he spurns, and Narcissus wastes away admiring his own reflection in the still water. Marcuse would respond that an untimely death is bound to be their fate in a repressive order. Orpheus and Narcissus can live only in a new world, utopia. It is worth remembering, Marcuse might add, that the value of utopia never depended upon its plausibility but on the way it speaks to our hidden desires, and so generates a critique of contemporary culture. Utopia has always done this, and it will help to consider another utopian vision of freedom before returning to Marcuse's.

"Meant to Do That" and Freedom

This other utopian vision is so familiar that it is hiding in plain sight. Briefly examining its origins and development will help bring it into relief. For Plato in the *Republic*, the utopian goal is not just to be master of oneself but to be immune to *tuche*, a term often translated as "chance" or "fate," the same fate to which both Carel the crazed cleric as well as my informants feel so exposed.[2] Here is the hidden (or perhaps not so hidden) agenda at the heart of the Western ideal of freedom: to render the self invulnerable to fate, generally by showing the world to be as one really wanted it to be all along. In other words, the Western ideal of freedom also draws on Narcissus, but on another aspect of our antihero, one at least as regressive as that praised by Marcuse. In the Western tradition, the aspect of Narcissus that is covertly idealized (or perhaps one should simply say unquestioned) is his refusal to put himself in a position to suffer narcissistic injury, as it is called—that is, an insult to one's pride or self-esteem. Narcissus cannot know that his will is not strong enough to subdue the world, that he remains subject to power and chance: the power of other people and the otherness of nature itself. Though they are far less subtle about it, young people want what Western philosophy has always wanted: to be *autokratôr*, master of one's fate. Will they turn narcissist to do it? Have they? Yes and no.

Summarizing the history of Western thought on freedom in a few thousand words is a big (indeed, impossible) task, and so I will begin with a small story told to me by my parents. When I was a toddler, just learning to walk, I would often stumble and fall. My coordination was not yet adequate to my will to walk. When I fell I would yell out "meant to do that, meant to do that." Then I would throw myself to the floor a couple of more times just to prove it. I would, in other words, try to take control of my limits by turning them into an intention. My goal, in other words, was not just to walk. It was to protect myself from narcissistic injury—that is, knowledge of my own weakness and dependence. Much Western thought on freedom seems to have the same goal.

If the following summary of Western thought on freedom seems cavalier, the reader should know it is intended merely to exemplify my perspective, a variation of Marcuse's, not to prove it. In any case, I make no claim to have captured the essence of Western thought about freedom in a few thousand words, only to have identified a single and surprising thread: freedom as defense against narcissistic injury, an injury to one's pride or self-esteem.

For Rousseau, freedom means liberation from the knowledge of one's terrible dependence on others. It is this that unites *The Second Discourse*,

Emile, and *The Social Contract*. The way this works for Emile was discussed previously. Emile's education is designed to foster the illusion that the limits imposed by his tutor are part of the objective determinism of nature. It is impossible to summarize *The Social Contract* here; however, the problem Rousseau is trying to solve is straightforward: how to restore to civilized men something of the freedom they enjoyed in the state of nature? Quite unlike Hobbes, Rousseau imagines the state of nature as a primitive idyll, men and women utterly autonomous and absolutely free, having no need for each other except for brief sexual encounters. How can this freedom be maintained in society?

Rousseau's answer, in *The Social Contract*, is that if I give myself up to all the other citizens—not to a leader and not to individuals but my fellow citizens as a whole—it is as though I give myself up to no one. If I want only what all the other citizens want, then I can be said to be free, for nothing and no one constrains me. Rousseau calls this agreement the "General Will," arguing that it restores the freedom of the noble savage by making it as if I give myself up to all I give myself up to none. "For such is the condition which, uniting every citizen in his Homeland, guarantees him from all personal dependence" (book 1, chapter 7). This guarantee is, of course, the point.

To be sure, in the very next chapter of *The Social Contract* (book 1, chapter 8), Rousseau argues that civil freedom is not just the reproduction but the improvement of natural freedom. Being forced to take others into account, the citizen becomes moral. If the general will does not truly restore the freedom of the noble savage, it nonetheless frees the citizen from constraint by identifying his will with that of all the others. If I will what all the others will, then they cannot constrain me, for it would be as though I were constraining myself, an insight that Kant will adopt.

For Rousseau, freedom means freedom from narcissistic humiliation, the knowledge that one is dependent on the will of others. It is in this freedom that Emile is to be raised. It is for the sake of this vision of freedom that the general will exists. Jean Starobinski (1988, xxii–xxiii) says that freedom for Rousseau is defined essentially as freedom from difference or otherness. If it is only the reality of others that reminds us of our constraints, eliminate otherness and we shall all be as free as the day we were born. This is the point of the general will.

In *Freedom's Moment: An Essay on the French Idea of Liberty from Rousseau to Foucault*, Paul Cohen (1997) argues that Rousseau began a particularly French way of thinking about freedom that continues to this day, one that equates freedom with the absence of personal dependence. The trouble with this view, Cohen continues, is that it has led the French to be insufficiently critical of anonymous sources of oppression, such as bureaucracy and the state. As long as one is not being oppressed by an identifiable individual, then one is free. Though Cohen must stretch mightily to make his argument fit Sartre and Foucault, it is true to the spirit of Rousseau, even if Rousseau did not have the French *bureaucrate* in mind when formulating the General Will. Fortunately, Cohen's observation is not true to the spirit of most people I talked with. Though many find personal dependence galling, most understand that the real threats to their freedom are anonymous, more likely to originate with one's HMO than with one's doctor or even senator.

For Immanuel Kant, human freedom is the freedom to accept objective reality, such as the laws of nature or the categorical imperative. Kant believes that the laws of this reality, which appear to be external to human beings, are actually unwitting projections of human reason. Thus, to accept these laws is equivalent to accepting what we ourselves have willed. "The will (*der Wille*) is a kind of causality belonging to living beings insofar as they are rational; freedom would be the property of this causality that makes it effective independent of any determination by alien causes" (Kant, 1981, 49). Though a part of me may rebel at the determination of these laws (a part Kant labels Willkür or arbitrary will), if I am rational I will accept these laws for I will know that I have made them. Is this so different from "meant to do that?"

Kant's view of freedom is described thus by Marcuse's Frankfurt School colleagues Max Horkheimer and Theodor Adorno (2002, 65–66).

> Kant intuitively anticipated what Hollywood has consciously put into practice: images are precensored during production by the same standard of understanding which will later determine their reception by viewers. The perception by which public judgment feels itself confirmed has been shaped by that judgment even before the perception takes place.

Horkheimer and Adorno wrote during the postwar era, in which movies were heavily censored for anything that might offend the public—or the censors. But the point remains valid. To call self-censorship freedom because it conforms to what one would have wanted anyway is to ignore the possibility that what one wants depends upon what one thinks one can have. Why would anyone restrict his or her imagination in this way? One reason is to protect the illusion of freedom. If I can't imagine having something, then I need not experience being deprived of it. I need not, in other words, experience my freedom as impotent.

For Hegel, freedom is being at home in the world through full possession of it (*zu Hause sein in der Welt*). To be free is to know that one would have made the world as it is, as one can deduce its present structure from objective principles. The dualism, or conflict, between individual morality and social institutions is only apparent. Modern institutions, such as family, civil society, and the state, do not require duties in conflict with my individual ends. Rather, these institutions are the realization of individual free will, an instance of compatibilism, as the doctrine is called. If one had known the course of history and if one had the power to change it, one would have made it the way it is. "What is rational is actual and what is actual is rational" (Hegel, 1967, 10). Is that not the world-historical version of "meant to do that"?

Hegel is nothing if not complex, for it is also Hegel (1967, 258A) who defines freedom as, "being at home with oneself in another" ("*bei sich selbst in einem anderen*"), a vision of freedom as the conjunction of independence and dependence that reminds one of Winnicott's transitional experience. In this famous formulation, Hegel avoids the poles of losing and fusing, positing a strictly non-borderline vision of freedom akin to "freedom with." Nevertheless, one must agree with Charles Taylor (1975, 373–375) that, in the end, freedom for Hegel is the freedom to bring one's own purposes into alignment with the purposes of the spirit that guides the world, what Hegel called *Geist*, his concatenation of God and History.

For Nietzsche (1968, 221), freedom is the will to power, which (as we have seen) has little to do with dominating others and everything to do with conquering all that is weak and base in oneself, so that one will have the strength to will what is. The will to power is the will to obliterate the presence of Orpheus and Narcissus within oneself, in so far as they represent passivity and the abandonment of mastery. "Amor fati," Nietzsche called it, the will to love one's fate, the will to wish it would never end. *Amor fati* is the philosophical version of "meant to do that," and Adorno was right to chide Nietzsche for it.

As different as these authors are, what unites them is a vision of freedom that aims to protect the narcissistic illusion that human autonomy and will are supreme, that constraint is not really constraint but a species of freedom. Horkheimer and Adorno (2002, 90) are perfectly clear about this, arguing that both Nietzsche's Overman and Kant's categorical imperative "aim at independence from external powers, at the unconditional freedom from tutelage which defines the essence of enlightenment." Sartre too participated in this aim, carving out a realm of being (or rather nonbeing), what he called *Néant*, which is absolutely free from external constraint. We imagine that freedom from tutelage is good, as it often is. Horkheimer and Adorno remind us how much freedom has depended upon self-censorship—that is, not wanting what one cannot have, a practice that only began with the Stoics.

While Plato's fascination with Socrates as the man who could never be harmed by anything that happened to him (*tuche*) must be considered the foundation of freedom as liberation from narcissistic injury, one should not overlook the Stoics. "Whoever wants to be free, therefore, let him not want or avoid anything that is up to others . . . You can be invincible if you do not enter any contest in which victory is not up to you" (Epictetus, *Handbook*, 14, 19). The Stoics too would render man free by virtue of *amor fati*: if you love your fate, then it is as though you freely chose it. If I love my fate enough, I can make myself totally free. What is so surprising is how much Western philosophy, from the most sublime (Kant) to the most apparently aggressive and self-assertive (Nietzsche), shares this defense, or perhaps we should call it therapy for humanity's wounded narcissism. Certainly Stoicism understood itself as therapy for the wounded soul.

The content of the healing insight varies enormously, of course, but for the philosophers considered above the basic idea remains the same. One heals the wounded self by liberating oneself from the point of view of the individual human—that is, you and me. Instead, one takes up the perspective of God, or whatever has become of God in the modern world: reason, history, community, or fate. Taking up a perspective outside oneself, it is as though one took on the powers of this outside as well. In a dozen different guises, the Western philosophy of freedom is Stoic.

To be sure, this generalization doesn't fit Nietzsche. On the contrary, Nietzsche calls for passionate involvement in one's life, and in this sense he does not share the Stoic strategy. Nevertheless, Nietzsche's passionate embrace of *amor fati* and the eternal return has much the same effect. Rather than pulling back from our fate and observing it from afar, Nietzsche asks that we identify with our fate, as though to love it. In so doing, we master fate not by ignoring it but by becoming it, a strategy opposite to that of the Stoics but with an identical goal. "Ignominious adaptation to one's prison" is not the only way to characterize Nietzsche's strategy, as Adorno did. Anna Freud (1966, 109–121) refers to the phenomenon she calls "identification with the aggressor," the tendency to fuse with a feared source of power in order to make it one's own.

Sigmund Freud's daughter was referring to the little boy's tendency to identify with his fearsome father, but she might as well have been referring to Nietzsche. The tendency of Western thought to conceive freedom as a defense of wounded will is but an instance of the larger tendency of Western thought to conceive of philosophy as defense of the beleaguered self. This is what Iris Murdoch (1966, 172) means when she says, referring to Carel's dark fears, that all philosophy has taught a facile optimism, too often purchased by teaching us to identify with the fate and power that causes us to suffer by turning these alien forces into expressions of human categories, such as reason or history.

Doesn't Marcuse do the same thing, the reader may be asking, in effect arguing that men and women will not be at home in the world until the world no longer requires our labor, until world Eros and human Eros unite? Isn't this identification with the aggressor too? Yes and no. Marcuse presents a vision of the world so infused with Eros that it becomes part of human nature, human nature a part of world nature. The opposition among men, women, and nature expressed in the need to labor will itself be overcome, and Eden will be restored. The difference is that Marcuse sets this goal in the utopian future not in the present. It hasn't happened yet. As it is, humans are deeply alienated from their own freedom, which is at its best a shrunken vestige of its potential. In other words, Marcuse does not imagine that we are already free, or that we just don't know it yet.

In the current circumstances, the claims of Orpheus and Narcissus are bound to express themselves regressively, the search for peace and contentment found not in life but death. The longings of Alcibiades and young people for sleep and relaxation reflect the truth of Orpheus and Narcissus, as well as the way this truth is tormented under the performance principle, as Marcuse (1966, 44) calls it: the stratification of society based upon competitive economic performance. In such a world, power and mastery are the currency of everyday life, sleep and relaxation a nocturnal retreat. Earlier, this experience of freedom was characterized as Epicurean freedom or rather as wanna-be Epicurean freedom. Wanna-be Epicurean freedom is Orphic freedom, defined not just by the release it seeks but by its sometimes silent rebellion against the demands of everyday life.

Recall that for many people not just sleep but relaxation is an activity of the night. Seven people went further, equating freedom with death. One put it this way. "I have so much to do, I feel like I'm working even when I'm asleep. I don't think I'll be free until I die. Then I'll have all the time I need." Gela laughed, but I think she'd scared herself.

Horkheimer and Adorno (2002, 26) describe this way of living as follows.

Humanity had to inflict terrible injuries on itself before the self—the identical, purpose-directed, masculine character of human beings—was created, and something of this process is repeated in every childhood. The effort to hold itself together attends the ego at all its stages, and the temptation to be rid of the ego has always gone hand-in-hand with the blind determination to preserve it . . . Deathlike sleep is one of the oldest social transactions mediating between self-preservation and self-annihilation, an attempt by the self to survive itself.

The desire of many people for relaxation, sleep, and a hot bath, a desire that they equate with a second freedom, so to speak, a freedom of the darkness, when the struggle for mastery ceases for a few hours, represents not just a desire for respite but the hidden desire of Western civilization to abandon the Promethean struggle for mastery, built as it is on a vain attempt to assuage the wounded will. This is probably how Horkheimer, Adorno, and Marcuse would interpret informants' responses. Civilization's hidden desire is Alcibiades' desire, to be passive like the stereotype of woman, to sleep like death, to abandon oneself to the rhythm of the soul.

Most people spoke of relaxation in terms of being alone, often at night, free of the demands of others. However, a number spoke of relaxation in social terms, relaxing with others with whom they are comfortable at the end of the day. For these people, conversation among friends is like sinking into a hot bath, liberating them from the self-monitoring that marks most of their waking and working hours. Peter compared this experience to the feeling he gets after working out at the gym. Paul compared the effect of a bottle of beer. "Sure, usually I have a few when I'm with my friends. But I don't need to. Just being with them is better than beer."

Equating the quest for mastery with the vain attempt to assuage the wounded will, Horkheimer and Adorno (2002) argue that not just economic competition but the otherness and intransigence of nature itself, which cares nothing for humans and their happiness, explains the attempts of idealistic and materialistic philosophies alike to assuage the will. That our will matters little against the forces of nature, including the second nature that is society, is just too hard for the bourgeois to bear. And in this regard, at least, we are all bourgeois. Even Nietzsche, whose *amor fati* is but another way of saying "meant to do that."

Marcuse's view is a little different. Wounded will is not so important as in my account, unless one believes that wounded will is transformed into aggression, the death drive that would destroy civilization. Certainly an aspect of this way of thinking is present in *Eros and Civilization*, Marcuse's (1966) reinterpretation of Freud's *Civilization and Its Discontents*. According to Marcuse, for the most part, however, it is not wounded will but denied pleasure that makes people hostile to civilization and so eager to take out their aggression on others.

Marcuse's account comes closer to the perspective of the informants than to my own. Both Marcuse and young people set the claims of Orpheus and Narcissus against the performance principle. The difference is that Marcuse thinks Orpheus and Narcissus might one day rule. Those I spoke with do not share this beautiful illusion (*schöner Schein*) as Marcuse calls it. For most people, Orpheus and Narcissus remain creatures of the night.

Though my interpretation and Marcuse's are not identical, they converge in the recognition that the alternative to the performance principle is a type of rhythmic attunement with the world. This rhythm is represented in myth not just by the lyre of Orpheus but also by the appeal of the Sirens to Odysseus and his men, an appeal that represents the desire to abandon oneself and return to a mythic unity with nature. Marcuse calls this desire freedom, though of course it is not quite that simple. Marcuse's ideal of freedom is not passivity and abandonment but an attunement with nature, including human nature, so that what is now such hard work becomes play. Passivity and abandonment are reactions against the performance principle not the alternative to it. Not passivity but rhythmic attunement with the world is Marcuse's ideal. Nowhere is this better captured than in Rainer Maria Rilke's *Sonnets to Orpheus.*

> Almost a maid, she came forth shimmering
> From the high happiness of song and lyre,
> And shining clearly through her veils of spring
> She made herself a bed within my ear
> And slept in me. All things were in her sleep:
> The trees I marveled at, the enchanting spell
> Of farthest distances, the meadows deep,
> And all the magic that myself befell,
> Within her slept the world.[3]

If one sees attunement as the alternative to the struggle for mastery, then Sartre's *Nausea* reads a little differently. Recall how Roquentin sought to overcome his nausea, the terrible feeling that the roots of the chestnut tree were about to swallow him up: by attempts at intellectual mastery, such as categorizing the trees. "In vain I tried to *count* the Chestnut trees . . . to compare their height with the height of the plane trees" (Sartre, 1964, 128, his emphasis).

Is there any alternative to this failed strategy of intellectual domination? One other possibility presents itself in *Nausea.* Attunement with his feelings of loss is another strategy by which Roquentin tries to deal with his malaise. "One of these days you'll miss me honey," sings the singer of Roquentin's favorite song, the song that he would play again and again because it allows him to feel the loss of Anny, who causes dark little tides to be born in his heart (Sartre, 1964, 22, 70). "Four notes on the saxophone. They come and they go, they seem to say: you must be like us, suffer in rhythm. All right! Naturally I'd like to suffer that way" (174). He can't quite, but he knows the cure. Absent the *feeling* of loss, Roquentin feels that he is about to be swallowed by things, the slimy contingency of the world. The experience of nausea is, it seems, the opposite of rhythmic, tuneful feeling. If so, then perhaps it is not *Néant* but tuneful feeling that is the realm of freedom. The way this works is "freedom with."

Is not Donovan's "Colours," quoted in chapter 2, an account of love that Orpheus would recognize? (Trouble is, it is an account of love that Orpheus would prefer, memory over reality.) Is not "in the groove" an Orphic image, reminding us of the beautiful music of his lyre? Not exactly. Orpheus is attuned to himself and nature. "In the groove" is attuned with others who make music, which is not quite the same thing. Here is the difference between "freedom with" and Marcuse's image of Eros, which seems in the end turned back on itself, even as Marcuse would surely argue that it cannot be, for it is through Eros that we join the natural world.

Repressive Tolerance

Repressive tolerance Marcuse (1965a) called it, the way in which freedom of expression not only fails to challenge the existing order but actually supports it. When everything is permitted then society is invulnerable, as everything can be taken in, tamed, and rendered harmless, transformed into an instance of "self-expression." Society incorporates everything. There is no longer any outside. The result is that speech is no longer powerful and dangerous but simply effete. It is this that many young people intuit so well. One can, they know, say anything and be ignored, which is why they view freedom of speech as an empty symbol.

Younger informants especially suffer under repressive tolerance. They actually expected to be free in the reality of their everyday lives, an outrageous and revolutionary thought that should turn the world upside down, especially when it dawns on them that it is not going to happen. But this dawn is a false dawn, or at least it doesn't lead to radical politics. Why? One might argue that it is because the content of the freedom they fear they will be denied is itself strictly conventional: money, power, and status. How does one mount a revolution to get these nonrevolutionary goods? One can refuse to play the game, but then you have to redefine what counts as winning. It's hard to refuse to play and yet want all the goodies that the game grants its winners. This is the situation many young people find themselves in. A number are paralyzed by the choice. "I can be a suit, or I can be a bum," says Michael. "That's why I'm so unambitious. I don't want either. My older sister says I'm lazy, but she wears a suit and she's miserable. Why should I want that?"

One wants to say that Michael lacks imagination, as though these were the only two choices in the world. That's part of the story but it's a little more complicated. Like the vast majority of people I spoke with, Michael does not believe in the ultimate value of money, power, and status. Nor do most believe that money, power, and status stand as proxies for higher values, such as excellence at one's profession. People know that teachers and nurses, for example, contribute much and generally get paid little. Like Michael, many young people simply cannot imagine alternatives to money and power that will protect them from the intrusions of others, the mortification of being subject to another's will, perhaps the gravest embarrassment of them all. Rousseau would understand. For many young people, it's win the game or die, and not just of embarrassment. Several people, all college students, imagined that if they did not succeed, they would wind up homeless, at risk of starvation, illness, and early death. It's hard to say their fear is entirely fantastic.[4]

Jack is thirty-something. He has traveled all over the world as a computer consultant, and recently returned to school. He lived in France for a while, and talks about a friend there who said, "We're just deeper than you [Americans] are." Jack agrees. Not because the French are smarter, or even better educated, but because they have more economic security.

"They don't have to worry so much about money or health care. They can spend more time developing themselves. My boss said 'where there's a will there's a way.' But too much will will get in the way of freedom. You can't just relax and listen." He means listen to other people talk and so learn something new. Jack's good at that.

One is tempted to see many young people as suffering from the psychological effects of repressive tolerance.[5] In regimes marked by repressive tolerance, authority is abstract and obscure, embodied not in fathers, teachers, and bosses but in "the bureaucracy," or "the system." The result is that there is no longer anyone to fight against and no point in fighting. If you can say anything and no one cares, if the barriers against your freedom are better characterized by terms such as "the system" instead of "my father," or "the ruler," then soon enough it becomes pointless to imagine how it might be otherwise. When there is no outside there is never any otherwise.

Raised in regimes marked by repressive tolerance, young people suffer from a lack of imagination, the realm of "otherwise." What Michel Foucault calls discipline, the focus of chapter 6, is similar: authority is invested not in individuals but in experts, such as doctors and lawyers, against whom it is hard to fight, since it seems as if one is fighting reason and knowledge itself.

There is a superficial resemblance between Marcuse's critique of the effects of repressive tolerance and that of conservative critics of freedom such as James Fitzjames Stephen (1975, 147), who writes, "if you wish to destroy originality and vigour of character, no way to do so is so sure as to put a high level of comfort easily within the reach of moderate and commonplace exertion." Doesn't this fit the young people I interviewed? Yes and no. Certainly they take for granted the great freedoms they do possess. On the other hand, consider the rest of Stephen's remark. "A life made up of danger, vicissitude, and exposure is the sort of life which produces originality and resource." Yes, the originality and resourcefulness of Odysseus and Alcibiades, based upon a way of living that requires the repression of vast tracts of the self's desire to relax and just be. Young people want freedom to be easy and plentiful and are angry that it is not. Marcuse teaches that there is hope in their naïve dissatisfaction. Some things are spoiled when you have to fight too hard and too long for them, and freedom as respite is one.

Although young people exhibit an utter lack of imagination regarding how society could be transformed, although they possess no sense of an alternative social order, there is an alternative present in their lives, one expressed in sleep and relaxation as experiences of freedom. In this second dimension of freedom as respite there is an alternative principle at work, one not too distant from that of Orpheus and Narcissus, to which many young people are open, even if only when the day's work is done. An inner space of freedom not defined by money and power but almost entirely split off from the concerns of the world, available generally only at the end of the day, is accessible to many people.

One is tempted to ask how experiences of relaxation could be rendered political. Wouldn't this reduce the distance between freedom as mastery and freedom as relaxation? Yes, and certainly there is something to the project. As Sheldon Wolin (2001, 464) observes, the "socialism" of the French revolution connoted not only the right to form producer and consumer cooperatives but also meant sociability, "sharing ideas, expressing grievances, and inventing strategies in a convivial setting." Recall that for many people, relaxation is social, about being with friends in noninstrumental ways. Consider Jack's answer to the question, "When are you most free?"

"When I'm in a coffee shop, discussing with anyone about anything. I get to break out of my own limits. I have to reevaluate myself, I can say what I want but I must reevaluate what I say. It's like getting a shot of adrenalin."

Before the fall of the Berlin Wall, some Eastern European countries were said to be characterized by "freedom of the coffee house." You could say almost anything you wanted, even in public, as long as the setting was social, among friends, and not political; in other words, as long as you did not challenge the regime. Authoritarianism with a human face, it might be called. Doesn't recent history demonstrate that there was political potential here too? Yes, and it would be a mistake to underestimate the political potential of sociability. Nevertheless, this is not my argument. Transforming relaxation into a political resource risks spoiling the experience, turning it into a means. That, or it risks trivializing the experience of relaxation, transforming it into a resource for the state, as much of the literature on civil society does. This is the focus of chapter 6.

Rather than focusing on the transformation of relaxation into a political resource, and so spoiling it, it seems more fruitful to focus on the other half of the split in freedom: how might mastery be rendered more political? In other words, how might people come to see that their legitimate desires for mastery and control over their own lives are not just an individual but a political project? This is the focus of chapters 5 and 6.

If people can experience a little more mastery and control over their own lives, then there will be space enough (they themselves will find it) to experience the second dimension of freedom, freedom as respite. For almost all, this will be a private space. To make freedom as respite a public affair not only risks spoiling the experience; it risks making freedom dangerous. The clearest *political* expression of freedom as respite is found in political movements that encourage the abandonment of the self to something larger and more transcendent. In politics this is hardly ever good.

Why Do Young People See the World as Carel the Crazed Cleric Does? And Why Doesn't President Bush?

That young people see the world in terms of power and fate is an empirical observation based upon interviews and discussion panels involving dozens of informants over a period of several years. That their dark vision leads them to devalue freedom for the sake of power, while longing for an Orphic respite from this struggle, is not an empirical observation but a conclusion drawn from things people say. Why the people I spoke with see the world this way must remain speculation, albeit speculation based upon what they say, as well as what they don't. The following remarks should be read with these considerations in mind.

An enormous increase in inequality has occurred over the last 30 years in the United States, the world in which young people have grown up. The result is that young people take inequality for granted, though inequality is perhaps not the right word. A vast disproportion between the rich and the rest of us comes closer to the mark, a disproportion that directly translates into a disproportion in freedom. Or so younger informants see it. The disproportion is not obvious when one looks at income distribution across quintiles and even deciles. The increase has been dramatic only at the very top 1 or 2 percent of the population. Anyone making over $81,000 per year is in the top 10 percent, but more than half of the gains in the share of the top 10 percent over the last 30 years went to the top 1 percent, and half of these gains were a mere 13,000 taxpayers, the top 0.01 percent, who had an average income of 17 million dollars.[6]

The figures soon become mind numbing, and it is not data but subjective economic experience that is our concern. Over the last 30 years, the average annual salary grew about 10 percent, adjusting for inflation. Most of this increase is accounted for by women working longer hours. During this same period, the compensation of the top 100 CEOs grew from 39 times the pay of the average worker to more than 1,000 times the pay of the average worker.[7] Young people don't generally know the numbers, but they have a good sense (the mass media see to that) that they live in a world in which a few live lives of extraordinary privilege while the rest of us struggle to pay the bills. ("Lifestyles of the Rich and Famous" was the real name of a popular television show that ran for several years.) For most, losing one's job means losing one's health insurance. In other words, losing one's job may be hazardous to one's health. For top CEOs, losing one's job means a lifetime of riches.

Writing about all this and more, Paul Krugman (2002) concludes that the "middle-class America of my youth is best thought of not as the normal state of our society, but as an interregnum between Gilded Ages, lasting from the New Deal through the 1970's." One might imagine that 1987 was the height of the new Gilded Age, bringing us the "Masters of the Universe," as the investment bankers in Tom Wolfe's *Bonfire of the Vanities* called themselves, as well as Gordon Gecko in the movie "Wall Street," who proclaimed that greed is good. But 1987 was only the beginning. Today the top 0.01 percent earn 60 percent more than they did in 1987.

What accounts for this change? Krugman posits a hypothesis that would have been considered "irredeemably fuzzy-minded not long ago.

This view stresses the role of social norms in setting limits to inequality." Sometime in the 1970s, a new permissiveness arose that can be compared to the sexual revolution of the 1960s. Only, in this case, the permissiveness is financial not sexual.

Young people know all this and more in their bones. We live in a New Gilded Age, in which the chance exists for a few to live like royalty, and it is these few who exemplify what freedom looks like in this world: the possession of enough money and power to go anywhere and do anything, a world without limits and boundaries. Or at least without someone telling you what to do. Putting it this way is actually more accurate, for it is not my impression that most young people are greedy for money and power. Rather, they are frightened that in a world of increasing inequality, only money and power will protect them from the impingement of others. It is hard to say that they are completely wrong about this. Young people experience themselves as living in a state of nature like that described by Thomas Hobbes, in which only power can defeat power. Not for a moment do they imagine that the power of the state will protect them. It is hard to say that they are wrong about this either.

Almost all the research of recent years reveals young people to be more economically conservative than their parents, especially as far as privatization is concerned. The younger the voter the more likely he or she is to favor privatizing Social Security (that great oxymoron), as well as to favor tuition tax vouchers.[8] This fits the results of my survey of younger informants, who are more likely to say that "the existence of some rich and some poor is compatible with a free society" than the respondents to the GSS, who represent a random, and hence older, population. (See the Research Appendix.) Often, it is argued that young people favor privatization because they are more selfish, or at least less community-minded, than their elders. It might be more accurate to say that they better understand how little the state will do to protect them.

Recall the young woman who defined freedom as being "the CEO of my own life." If top CEOs earn 1,000 times more than the average worker, one can see the attraction. Not just the attraction of the material goods that money can buy but the attraction of actually becoming *autokratôr*, a state unto oneself in a world in which the state cannot be relied upon for protection. One might respond that young people fail to appreciate the protection they do receive from the state, the protections that can be summarized under the rubric constitutionalism. This criticism is just, as is argued in chapter 7. Nonetheless, the material world in which young people have grown up does little to relieve them of the impression that they have been abandoned in the "empire of might," as

Simone Weil puts it. It is the experience of being a citizen of this empire that frames young people's experiences of freedom, both the equation of freedom with power as well as the longing for respite from the quest for power, which is also freedom for so many people.

This is not President George W. Bush's world, and it is certainly not the world he grew up in. In Bush's case, embraced rather than abandoned by the empire of might comes closer to the mark. If freedom is not just an ideal but a complex refraction of one's material reality, then it is not surprising that little of what Bush says about freedom resonates with the young people I interviewed. Still, it is interesting to consider whether anything we have said so far can illuminate the American president's fascination with freedom. In his *New York Times* op-ed piece, "Securing Freedom's Triumph," published on the first anniversary of the terrorist attacks of September 11, 2001, an essay that runs just a little over a thousand words, Bush uses the terms free or freedom 21 times.

The issue will not, however, be settled by counting words. What needs to be explained is the way in which freedom becomes an almost universal explanation for the president, as when Bush suggests that the terrorists who beheaded Nicholas Berg did so because they hate freedom. Just a few months earlier, Bush explained the Iraq war in this way. "There are terrorists there [Iraq] who would rather kill innocent people than allow for the advance of freedom. That's what you're seeing going on: these people hate freedom and we love freedom."[9]

Nor is Bush's interest in freedom confined to the Iraq war. In his January 2002 State of the Union Address, Bush proposed that the Peace Corps, Americorps, and half a dozen other programs be brought together under something called the Freedom Corps. Clearly freedom lies close to the president's heart. The question is what meaning does his heart give to freedom?

One might argue that for Bush freedom has lost its magic. Instead of identifying a transitional space in which we are free to depend on others without constantly being reminded of that fact, instead of possessing that almost magical quality called "freedom with," in which we allow boundaries to become obscure, freedom becomes the opposite principle, a way to sharply divide the world into good and bad. Freedom is, in other words, both the principle of division and the goodness that remains safely in one's hands after the division is complete. For Bush, freedom is the opposite of a transitional relationship and the "freedom with" that goes with it.

And yet it seems that one could say the converse and also be correct. For in another sense, freedom is already far too magical for Bush, having the quality of an everything that is nothing, something so valuable and powerful that we do not have to do anything except invoke its name as though it were a magical incantation, as though the word itself had magical powers to bring itself to life. To be sure, from time to time Bush invokes the cliché, "freedom is not free," as he did when announcing an initiative under which American war veterans would share their experiences with schoolchildren in order to illustrate the price of defending democracy.[10] All in all, however, Bush has asked little of Americans in the days since September 11, 2001, except of course of those who serve in the military.

This interpretation would fit the religious interpretation, so influential among intellectuals, who see in Bush a true believer, one who sees in Christian America God's chosen people, ordained to bring the blessings of liberty to others. Though the editors of *The Wall Street Journal* do not, of course, agree, they too acknowledge the influence of this interpretation.

> "These are times in which we could literally change the world by the spread of freedom," President Bush told supporters last week at a Wisconsin rally. "Freedom is not America's gift to the world; freedom is the Almighty God's gift to each man and woman in this world." In such declarations—and they are frequent from Mr. Bush—critics see a "messianic militarist" at work, to borrow a phase from Ralph Nader. (Loconte, 2004)

Finally, and to make things still more complicated, it would be unfair to ignore the fact that Bush has a fairly well thought out secular theory of political freedom, what he calls a "forward strategy of freedom in the Middle East." In a speech delivered at the National Endowment for Democracy, Bush pointed out that 60 years of Western nations excusing and accommodating the "lack of freedom in the Middle East did nothing to make us safe—because in the long run, stability cannot be purchased at the expense of liberty." It is in this context that he spoke about bringing pressure to bear on the Saudis, Egyptians, and others, to respect the liberties of their citizens. Bush likes to compare this aspect of his forward strategy for freedom to Reagan's continued rhetorical assault on the Soviet Union.

> Even though at the time many liberals worried that Reagan's bellicose language would increase the chances of nuclear confrontation, it turned out that his moralistic comments about Soviet-style tyranny helped encourage dissent in Eastern Europe and Russia itself. This is the model that Bush is trying to follow by fanning the flames of freedom, or at least a few embers of liberty, in the Middle East. It is hard to argue with the

president's assertion that "For too long, many people in that region have been victims and subjects. They deserve to be active citizens." But it is also proper to worry that these bold presidential words may be accompanied by continued American wink-and-a-nod tolerance of authoritarian regimes in the name of the war on terrorism. (Shapiro, 2003)

There are simply too many pieces of the president's use of the term freedom to put together, and perhaps that is the point. Though the most obvious and compelling thing to say about Bush's use of the term "freedom" is that it is employed in order to divide the world into black and white, and so bring simplicity to complexity, not even Bush's use of the term is that simple.

What one can say is that under pressure, and the pressure need not be intense, Bush seems to use the term "freedom" in an almost magical fashion, in which the principle of division itself becomes the source of all goodness and light. And while Bush's psychology and biography would certainly explain much in this regard, there is something about the experience of freedom that lends itself to this new Manichaeism, in which the sword that divides becomes the bountiful breast that provides, but only to those who truly love the goddess Freedom. This is, of course, a particularly borderline conception of freedom, but in this there is nothing new or unique.

CHAPTER 5
FREEDOM IS SEEING
REALITY CLEARLY

The simplest thing to say about Iris Murdoch is that she disagrees with almost everything Sartre says about freedom. One might imagine that she would disagree with almost everything Marcuse says as well. Probably she wouldn't. Marcuse's Frankfurt School colleague, Theodor Adorno, was an inspiration to Murdoch. What Marcuse might say about Murdoch I leave to the end of this chapter.

For Murdoch, freedom has nothing to do with what Sartre calls *Néant*, the imaginary negation of reality, and everything to do with seeing reality as clearly as one can. For Murdoch, *Néant* is narcissism. Freedom is knowing reality as truly and honestly as one can. One question we shall have to ask is whether seeing reality clearly has anything to do with freedom, even if one agrees with Murdoch that seeing reality clearly is desirable.

Not as well known as Sartre or Marcuse, Iris Murdoch, who died in 1999, is probably best known to Americans by virtue of the recent movie, "Iris," which follows her descent into Alzheimer's disease. Author of 26 novels, Murdoch taught philosophy at Oxford for many years. Often regarded as a Platonist in her philosophy, it is hardly obvious what it means to follow Plato these days. One might better label Murdoch a follower of Plato's teacher, Socrates. Certainly Murdoch saw herself that way. "Like Socrates," she said, "love is the only subject on which I am really expert" (Conradi, 2001a, xviii). Another question we shall have to ask is what love has to do with freedom. Quite a lot, as it turns out.

For Sartre, against whose view of freedom Murdoch (1987) developed her own, freedom is built on a paradox. In one's consciousness one is completely free, and yet this freedom is empty, without content and void. To practice our freedom, we must insert ourselves into the world with all its limits and constraints. In other words, to practice our freedom we must lose it, though never completely. For Murdoch, we are born into a world in which there was never an opportunity to stand back and choose our values. The task comes closer to learning what our values really are, but that is not quite right either. The task is to refine our values in light of our experiences and our experiences in light of our values.

One way to characterize Murdoch's vision of freedom is in terms of the debate over the "situated" or "encumbered" self that characterizes so much of contemporary social philosophy. For exponents of the situated or encumbered self, such as the political philosopher Michael Sandel, the self is defined by its enduring attachments and commitments. In order to explain this idea, Sandel (1996, 65–67) turns to the discussion of religious freedom among the leaders of the American Revolution. For Thomas Jefferson, freedom of religion didn't mean the freedom to choose this or that religion. It meant the freedom to stick with the religion with which one is encumbered. About things such as religion, there is no free choice, only the freedom to stick with those beliefs that one is stuck with. Or as Jefferson put it, "the opinions and beliefs of men depend not on their own will, but follow involuntarily the evidence proposed to their own minds." In putting it this way, Jefferson echoes his muse, John Locke, who argued in *A Letter Concerning Toleration*, "it is absurd that things should be enjoined by laws which are not in men's power to perform. And to believe this or that to be true, does not depend on our will" (quoted in Sandel, 1996, 65).

If this is so, then do we want to say that men and women are free, at least as far as such basic values as religious belief are concerned? We may, but only if we decide that freedom has little to do with choosing between one value and another. Instead, freedom is the freedom to act in accordance with the values one already possesses—or perhaps one should say in accordance with the values by which one is possessed.[1]

Maria Antonaccio (2000, 9) compares Murdoch with Sandel, arguing that for both "we are not 'unencumbered' selves who originate our own moral claims, but members of a community bound by moral ties antecedent to our choices." Yet, there is a decisive difference between Murdoch and those who hold to the encumbered self, such as Sandel. For Murdoch, humans are capable of evaluating and improving upon their unchosen commitments, via a process that Murdoch calls "unselfing," which is not quite so dramatic as it sounds. There is nothing like this in Sandel, who treats our encumbrances as sacred trusts rather than realities about which we should be suspicious.

A story will help explain Murdoch's view. Imagine, says Murdoch, a mother reflecting on her son's choice of a wife. The mother feels hostile toward her daughter-in-law, whom she finds common and unpolished, lacking in dignity and refinement. Her son, she is sure, has married beneath himself. The mother, always correct, nonetheless behaves cordially toward her daughter-in-law. Time passes, and mother decides it is time to reevaluate her position. Her daughter-in-law, she discovers, is not really vulgar but refreshingly simple, not undignified but spontaneous. The mother's conduct never changed; she was always and continues to be perfectly correct. But the mother has gone on a moral journey, a pilgrimage of the soul (Murdoch, 1970, 17–23).

The question of whether the mother's new vision of her daughter-in-law is, in fact, more accurate does not arise for Murdoch. At stake is not the correspondence of the mother's vision with some objective reality, but the ability of the mother-in-law to overcome narcissism and convention, and so see the other person more clearly. Instead of the term narcissism, Murdoch uses the term neurosis, but she means the same thing. Neurosis refers to fantasies that "inflate the importance of the self and obscure the reality of others." Convention refers to the tendency of the individual to become "sunk in a social whole which we allow uncritically to determine our reactions, or because we see each other exclusively as so determined" (1999a, 216). Both narcissism and convention acted as barriers to the mother-in-law's perception of her daughter-in-law, though in what combination it is impossible to tell.

"The enemies of art and of morals, that is the enemies of love, are the same: social convention and neurosis" (1999a, 216). Both obscure our vision of the particular other, what Murdoch calls attention, a term she draws from Simone Weil "to express the idea of a just and loving gaze directed upon an individual reality" (Murdoch, 1970, 34). "Love is the perception of individuals. Love is the extremely difficult realisation that something other than oneself is real" (Murdoch, 1999a, 215). The goal is to see the other person justly, honestly, and compassionately. Doing so means moving away from universality and principles and toward increasing depth, privacy, and particularity. "The central concept of morality, says Murdoch, is 'the individual' thought of as knowable by love" (1970, 30).

Is Murdoch just borrowing a term from Weil or is she borrowing a whole way of thinking? It is hard to tell. For Weil (1977d, 49), attention (*l'attention*) means to suspend thinking, leaving one's mind detached, empty, ready to be entered by the other. Attention means not always trying to know, not categorizing, but waiting, as though the other could participate in forming the idea we have of it. Attention is the opposite of a thought that has seized upon some idea too hastily, and thinks it knows. For Weil, attention is preparation for an encounter with God. For Murdoch, attention is the way we open ourselves to the experiences of other humans. But perhaps these are not so different after all. In the legend of the Holy Grail, the vessel belongs to the seeker who first asks its guardian, a king paralyzed by a painful wound, "What are you going through?" (Weil, 1977d, 51). That is paying attention. The question, of course, is what it might have to do with freedom.

"The highest love is in some sense impersonal," continues Murdoch. Not in the Kantian sense, which prefers good will to attachment. Love remains "the general name of the quality of attachment" (Murdoch, 1970, 75, 103). What is wanted is a quality of attachment that sees the imperfections of self and other clearly and still loves. Murdoch finds the epitome of this love in great art. "The realism of a great artist is not a photographic realism, it is essentially both pity and justice" (Murdoch, 1970, 87). Pity and justice not just for the subject, she might have added, but for the human race.

Transcend comes from the Latin (*transcendo*), meaning to climb over or go beyond the limits of something. Murdoch's goal is to go beyond the limits of the self. That is freedom. Not so much freedom from the self, but from the self's clinging attachment to itself and to social convention. It is no wonder that Murdoch became fascinated with Buddhism in her later years (Conradi, 2001a, 544–546).

"It is in the capacity to love, that is to *see*, that the liberation of the soul from [narcissistic] fantasy consists. The freedom which is a proper human goal is the freedom from fantasy, that is the realism of compassion" (Murdoch, 1970, 66–67). Why does Murdoch associate freedom from fantasy with compassion? For the same reason the Greek tragic poets did. How could a human being look truly at this world for even one moment and not feel compassion for his or her fellow sufferers?

If, as Murdoch holds, the central concept of morality is the individual as knowable by love, then Murdoch is a liberal. Not in the contemporary political sense but in the older classical sense of holding that it is the individual who is the source of value, the one truly sublime being in this world (1999b, 282). Yet, the sources of Murdoch's liberal vision include not only Weil but also Adorno, who argues that we must give ourselves over to the other if we are to truly know the other. "The subject is the object's agent, not its constituent," says Murdoch, quoting Adorno (Murdoch, 1992, 379; Adorno, 1978). If that is liberalism, it is not your garden variety, as it puts the reality of the other person first.

To be sure, Murdoch must stretch to incorporate Adorno into her vision, arguing that she deploys "Adorno's metaphysical ideas against his Marxist ideas" (378). One might respond that she would have been better off proceeding the other way around. Be that as it may, Murdoch's liberal vision is subtle and complex, inspired less by the liberty of the individual and more by awe, what might well be called love for particularity and otherness, an awe that doesn't fit very well with her Platonism, as both Murdoch and her critics have noted (Conradi, 2001a, 493).

But Is It Really Freedom?

For Murdoch, freedom *is* seeing the reality of other people clearly, though the term seeing could be misleading were we to take it literally, as some kind of objective perception. By seeing, Murdoch means the vision of the artist. "He sees the earth freshly and strangely but he is ultimately part of it, he is inside the things he sees and speaks of as well as outside them. He is of their substance, he suffers with them" (Conradi, 2001b, 17). Even the least creative may become artists in this sense, artists of everyday living.

Why is seeing clearly freedom, the puzzled reader may ask, and not something else, such as knowledge? This is the most important question. Freedom, after all, is not every good thing. The answer is that for Murdoch there is no outside to transcend to, and no inner citadel in which one can be free of attachment. There is reality with all its constraints, and there is narcissism, fantasy, and self-deception. That's it. Even will is just one more narcissistic way of seeing and not the most important.[2] Not will, but fantasy, self-deception, and social cowardice are the leading barriers to seeing clearly. To see reality clearly means to escape the bonds of illusion. That is freedom for Murdoch, the only freedom there is in this world.

There is a third barrier to seeing clearly that Murdoch does not mention in her philosophy but is important in her novels. One might call it obsessive attachment, a need for others so intense that it gets in the way of seeing them, or ourselves, clearly. Charles Arrowby, protagonist of Murdoch's *The Sea, the Sea* (1978), holds his long-lost girlfriend, Hartley, a prisoner in his country house. One might argue that this represents the power of egoism or narcissism, but it seems more a sign of his utter dependence upon her to keep from going insane. In her novels, but not in her philosophy, Murdoch recognizes the power of our terrible need for others. Not vanity but the insufficiency of the ego, its terrible need to find its other half, spoils relationships, turning them into tyrannies. Not just love but hate may have the quality of obsessive attachment, our need for our enemies being so strong we cannot do without them. Of course, it is a fine line between obsessive attachment and our profound and profoundly normal dependence on others. Nevertheless, Murdoch's novels are filled with characters who abandon themselves to others, and this is surely as much a barrier to seeing clearly as narcissism and convention.

It would be a mistake to argue that freedom for Murdoch means freedom *from* the self. She is not *that* Buddhist. Freedom is freedom from the delusions and obsessions of the self so that one's self is released into the world of others, not to be obsessed with them but to live with them. This release is freedom. "Techniques of unselfing" are the way in which one enters and remains within the reality of other beings.

> This is the non-metaphysical meaning of the idea of transcendence . . . the attempt to pierce the veil of selfish consciousness and join the world as it really is. It is an empirical fact about human nature that this attempt cannot be entirely successful. (Murdoch, 1970, 93)

And how is this world? It is the world of the unself, filled with particular others who are "to an extent we never cease discovering, different from ourselves" (1999a, 216).

By techniques of unselfing, Murdoch means nothing esoteric, referring instead to mundane experiences of nature and art, intellectual studies, such as learning a language, and paying attention to other people. Imagine, says Murdoch, the experience of looking out of the window in an anxious and resentful state, brooding on same damage to my prestige. "Then suddenly I observe a hovering kestrel. In a moment everything is altered. The brooding self with its hurt vanity has disappeared. There is nothing now but kestrel. And when I return to thinking of the other matter it seems less important" (1970, 84). In a similar way, intellectual studies (a category Murdoch considers in terms of Plato's *techné*), such as learning a language, confront one with

> an authoritative structure which commands my respect . . . My work is a progressive revelation of something which exists independently of me. Attention is rewarded by knowledge of reality. Love of Russian leads me away from myself towards something alien to me, something which my consciousness cannot take over, swallow up, deny or make unreal. (1970, 89)

The question is so important I must repeat it. Why is this freedom and not something else, such as awareness? Because we are so deeply situated in the world, what Sandel calls encumbered, that there is no transcendence except to know this, a knowledge that is as emotional as it is empirical. The empirical world with all its constraints is the realm of freedom, the only realm there is. To know this world, liberated from the false comforts of narcissism, convention, and obsessive attachment, is to enter into the realm of freedom, and so be liberated from all the ways in which we lie to ourselves.

Of course, not everyone sees the world in the same way. Another mother-in-law, having gone on her own pilgrimage, might conclude that her daughter-in-law really is shallow and vapid. Everything from genes to family to society to culture to personal experience influences our seeing. Bracketing or suspending narcissism, convention, and obsessive attachment as best as we can is more likely to bracket the things that cause us to see in ways *similar* to others rather than differently. That's the point of convention, after all, to see things as everyone else does. Similarly, narcissists are not noted for the uniqueness of their perceptions. "It's all about me" isn't unique, it is just selfish.

For Murdoch, seeing clearly is as much about moral imagination as it is moral effort. Indeed, in a certain sense the image of seeing is misleading, as it has misled Western epistemology for two millennia, as if knowledge of reality were available to all who would but look. To see clearly requires enormous imagination and creativity, not just to empathize with others but to grasp what is so simple that it is almost incomprehensible—how different other people are from ourselves and how similar too. To know both at the same time is the simplest and most difficult thing in the world, which is why it takes an artist of everyday living to do it.

If other people are more different from me than I imagine, then presumably other people are far more different from each other than we imagine. If so, then it is not surprising that they would see reality differently even—or rather especially—when the veils of narcissism, convention, and obsessive attachment are lifted. Seeing clearly is an epistemological concept as much as it is a moral one, but it is not a version of the correspondence theory of truth.

Consider the well-known story told by Sartre (1999, 42–43) about a young man who cannot decide whether to join the resistance. His brother had been killed by the Germans and his father was a collaborationist on bad terms with the young man's mother, who lives only for the young man. He is her sole care and support. Should the young man make his way to England, join the resistance, and revenge his brother in the full knowledge that he may be killed before he even reaches England? Or should he stay in France and care for his mother?

For Sartre there is no right answer, and it is hard to disagree with him, though Sartre seems mistaken when he says that he has nothing of use to tell the young man. Sartre may have nothing to tell the young man, but the young man might find it of inestimable value were someone to listen to him. Listening to himself talk, the young man might come to recognize his own values and so be better able to choose based upon true attention and love.

Still, it is hard to say that there is one answer more in accord with loving attention than another. Perhaps the right answer depends on the quality of the young man's relationship to his mother, and only he can know that, even if others may help him discover it, pointing out, for example, what seem like wrong answers—that is, answers couched strictly in the language of convention, such as "Everyone has an obligation to avenge his brother's death" or "A mother always comes first."

One wants to say that Murdoch carves out a position that allows men and women room in which to put themselves together in their own unique way, so as to make something out of what has been made of them, as Sartre puts it. It would be more accurate to say that Murdoch reinterprets what it means to be socially situated, what Sandel calls the encumbered self. Socially situated does not mean defined by one's social situation and commitments. Socially situated might better be called socially knowledgeable and related, in which the self is emotionally tuned-in to its world. The goal is to become more finely tuned, so that the self knows what it most cares about and is not so inhibited or constrained that it is unable to act on this basis.

Could one see this world clearly and not act accordingly? That is, is freedom just about seeing—that is, knowledge not acting? No. For Murdoch, one cannot see accurately but fail to act because the type of knowledge involved in seeing is emotional knowledge that is already a type of action. Martha Nussbaum's example of Peter and Joan shows why. (About love, Nussbaum and Murdoch are on the same wavelength.) Imagine, says Nussbaum (1990, 41), that Peter is the most important person in the world for Joan. You know this because she has told you this many times over lunch. Suddenly Peter dies, and Joan just goes on with her life, hardly pausing to go to the funeral. You would have to say (unless you think Joan was lying) that Joan does not yet really know that Peter has died, and that it will take a while for the knowledge to sink in. When it does she will be devastated.

Certain types of knowledge, it appears, are inseparable from our emotional response. Or rather, our emotional response *is* knowledge, albeit a particularly disturbing type of knowledge. Not just because it often brings bad news but because it challenges the sanctum sanctorum of my freedom: the freedom to give the facts the meaning I choose. "The world enters into the self as emotion, with enormous power to wound or heal," says Nussbaum (2001, 78). There is no space, no *Néant*, insulated from the upheaval that emotions bring to one's life.

One could argue that this means that the self is caused, determined, by its emotional experience, but that would be the wrong language, the language of things in motion. Not caused but contacted and communicated with by a world beyond one's skin, is the experience both Nussbaum and

Murdoch are talking about. Too often, the question is posed as one of free will versus causal determinism, as though we were completely free unless our behavior is caused as though we were objects in motion. Even Sartre in *Being and Nothingness* (1956) assumes that consciousness is either causally determined or absolutely free, as though emotional meaning did not have its own symbolic logic of liberation and constraint.

The trouble with being attuned to one's emotional experiences of the world is that it hurts. What we want from the world is not just emotional knowledge but what is called by that lovely French word *soulagement*: relief, support, and comfort for the soul in the face of one's terrible aloneness in the world.[3] The world can be a terrible place; being attuned to this reality is not necessarily a comfort. Most terrible of all, perhaps, is the loss of meaning, the horrifying thought that one must live one's life in a world governed by power and chance. About any philosopher, says Murdoch, the question we should ask is, "What is he afraid of?" (1970, 72). It is not just philosophers who are afraid. The crowding out of meaning, including the meaning of freedom, by power and chance seems to be the leading fear of many young people, even if most don't know it as fear but simply as reality.

In the absence of *soulagement*, one is tempted to find one's freedom in its simulacrum, such as power, either one's own or the result of fusion with a powerful group. A young man said that upon joining the Nazi Party he felt free for the first time in his life. How could this be? The answer is simple. Fusion with power is *soulagement*, an experience readily confused with freedom, as both experiences bring with them similar emotions of relief, abandonment of the burden of oneself, and power, experiences that have the quality of transcendence. (This is why, by the way, freedom as respite is properly an individual rather than a political ideal.)

Emotional attunement is not freedom. Acting in accord with one's deepest values *is* freedom. Emotional attunement allows us to act on the basis of our deepest commitments by helping us distinguish between real and superficial values, between ideals and idols. Emotional attunement allows us the possibility of acting on our deepest commitments if we are fortunate enough to live in a world that is not too hostile to action. Even then, there are generally opportunities for action, as Sartre reminds us.

About Murdoch's view of freedom, Antonaccio (2000, 97) says, "freedom consists of choosing within a moral world that is already structured by degree of value, rather than seeking to transcend this world by a creative leap of will." I would put it just a little differently. Freedom consists in joining this world whose structure has structured us too. We do so by trying to see the world as clearly as possible.

Where are the people I talked with in all this? Few talked about freedom in terms of emotional attunement to self and others, though there were exceptions. One was Sue, who said, "I feel free when I'm with a group of people who can relate to what I say, who can carry on a conversation. Then I don't have to monitor myself all that time. That's what I mean by free." Overall, my sense was neither that evaluative freedom was beyond the ken of young people nor that the concept was impossibly subtle. Being true to themselves and others, when it was on the agenda at all (as it was for perhaps a quarter of the informants), was a luxury reserved for a better time and place. As John put it, "I'd like to stop and feel the world around me. Listen to my kids, spend time with my friends. That's freedom too. I just don't have the time. Right now I have to make money and get an education. Maybe someday . . ."

One might locate John's response under the category of "convention," money and education being just two more defenses against seeing clearly. That would not be a mistake, but it would miss the irony (always so close to tragedy) of those young people who know they are trapped in conventional roles but see no way out, because they can conceive of no alternative. The great advantage of Murdoch's perspective is that it changes the rules of what counts as an alternative: neither money and power nor sleep and relaxation but opening one's eyes to the world around us. It's terribly difficult, of course, for all one has to do is look, the hardest thing in the world, primarily because there is so little comfort in it— neither the reassurance of money nor the consolation of sleep. To see clearly one does not need to be powerful but one has to be awake.

Young people experience themselves as being wide-awake, which is why so many want to go back to sleep. For these young people, being wide-awake means looking at reality without blinking, forcing oneself to stare into Carel's dark cupboard, where force and fate rule the world, where freedom is a luxury compared to money and power. Isn't that what wide-awake means?

Yes, but being wide-awake and seeing clearly are not the same. Being wide-awake means adopting the attitude of the self-made man on the make, the one who says "I know how the world really works, so don't try to put one over on me." Seeing clearly means not so much seeing through or seeing past the reality of everyday life, but seeing all the spaces and places within everyday life where alternative ways of living and being, what the great theorist of freedom John Stuart Mill called "experiments in living," are possible. While mass society in the United States has the quality of what Herbert Marcuse (1964) called one-dimensionality, in which there seems to be no way out, no alternative but marginalization and even starvation, this is itself an illusion. The United States is only one-dimensional at the level of mass society. All around us are people experimenting with their lives. We shall meet several in the next two chapters. We have already caught a glimpse of them, young people who find their truest freedom in the middle of the night, when everyone else is asleep, and they can stretch out in the darkness and for a few moments just be.

Is There Any Room Left for Politics?

To share in self-rule, says Sandel,

> Requires that citizens possess, or come to acquire, certain qualities of character, or civic virtues . . . The republican conception of freedom, unlike the liberal conception, requires a formative politics, a politics that cultivates in citizens the qualities of character self-government requires. (1996, 5–6)

With the term "republican conception of freedom," Sandel refers to a version of positive freedom that argues I am free only when I participate with others in my own governance, generally through the associational life of the community, such as participating in the local Rotary Club, PTA, and town council. While Murdoch certainly writes about character and self-formation, one might argue that her vision is so private that it is not relevant to politics. That would be mistaken, though her view of freedom changes the way we think about politics.

Freedom as seeing clearly is primarily a private affair, the project of the individual's moral pilgrimage, a journey in which political participation is not likely to play the central role for most people. Yet, the process by which the claims of narcissism, convention, and obsessive attachment are mitigated by republican political practice (i.e., associating with others) resembles the way they are mitigated in private life, a process of coming to terms with the separate reality of other people, so like oneself in some respects, and so different in others. In other words, republican practices resemble, albeit on a larger, cruder, and generally less subtle scale, the practices that promote freedom in individuals' lives. What more could one ask of politics than this?

One could ask that politics address the destructive effects of mass culture, the way in which mass culture fosters narcissism and conventionalism at once, and so makes seeing clearly almost impossibly difficult for many citizens who have no refuge from the culture. Rather than republican remedies for republican diseases, as Tocqueville refers to participation in the associational life of the community, a cultural critique along the lines of that mounted by the Frankfurt School of Critical Theory, or the similar critique of the French poststructuralists, such as Pierre Bourdieu (1993), is called for. Needed, in other words, is the critique of a way of life that presents narcissistic self-aggrandizement as the conventional wisdom, indeed as the end of history. Ideology critique once again becomes a central strategy in the pursuit of freedom and education its leading tactic.

Freedom, says Winston Smith in Orwell's *Nineteen Eighty-Four*, means being able to say that $2 + 2 = 4$. Smith lives in a totalitarian regime in which he is tortured by O'Brien until he can see that the answer is 5, or whatever the party says the answer is (1949, 209). In such a regime, freedom is stating the simple truth, such as slavery is not freedom. Is Murdoch's ideal, "seeing reality clearly," a version of Winston Smith's simple truth? Yes and no. For many people, the problem is that they see reality too clearly. They see the simple truth, that power and fate rule the world, but not the more subtle truth: that it could be otherwise. Even within an iron cage whose bars are made of power and fate there are small spaces in which to create new truths. Once again, the image of "seeing" is misleading, at least when taken literally. Not seeing but insight, which requires something like the inner space Sartre calls *Néant*, is needed. Not perhaps as much *Néant* as Sartre imagined, but just enough to play in.

Murdoch's fondness for Adorno's "metaphysics," which includes Adorno's fierce distaste for what he once called the wild self-assertion (*verwilderte Selbstbehauptung*) of liberal individualism, suggests one way of thinking about her political theory. "The primacy of the object," Adorno's main philosophical tenet according to Murdoch (1992, 373), means both respect for the other person's otherness and caring for the other, assignments that may be in tension, but are by no means incompatible. The liberal welfare state is a state of constant conflict, but it is no oxymoron.

A more interesting way of thinking about Murdoch's politics is one inspired by Herbert Marcuse (1978), who argues that it is the bourgeois novel that is the most radical document around. Not social realism, but the artistic revelation of society's inability to tame the power of Eros, and the promise of happiness beyond the bounds of reason that Eros represents, is the truly revolutionary political text. *Madame Bovary* is exemplary.

One imagines that Marcuse would find much to admire in Murdoch's novels, above all the way so many of her characters live and die for Eros. The title of *The Black Prince* (1975), in which 58-year-old Bradley falls crazily in love with 20-year-old Julian, refers to the dark side of Eros, the way it can come so close to death. If, however, one imagines what Marcuse might say about Murdoch the philosopher, then his judgment would be harsher. Not because Murdoch sees reality clearly, even ruthlessly, but for her inability to imagine that it could be *ganz anders*, completely different.

Yet, to render Murdoch a novelist of Eros does not seem quite right either; or rather, the Eros about which Murdoch writes is not the same as Marcuse's. In spite of her incredibly erotic private life (according to Conradi, 2001a), it is not always, or even usually, the Eros that shatters social bonds about which Murdoch writes. More commonly, it is the Eros that creates little family-like communities, frequently composed of school comrades who remain friends for a lifetime. Sometimes, as in *The Book and the Brotherhood* and *The Message to the Planet*, the group is organized around a guru, but the ties that bind each to the others are manifold. About such a vision, one could argue that it is completely unpolitical. Indeed, Conradi (2001a, 499) suggests that it is this that accounts for Murdoch's success as a novelist. "Postwar England increasingly rejected the good society in favour of the good relationship, isolating the self as the main site left for significant change."

What this judgment ignores is that Murdoch's little communities are not just liberal but enchanted, animistic, filled with an Eros that is more likely to charm the everyday world for a moment than to shatter it. In *The Green Knight* (1993, 485), small objects, such as stones, are physically attracted to the fey Moira, but only until she is old enough and ready to take her place in society. For Moy, the gain is barely worth the loss.

In the end, Murdoch is a critic of rationalization and mass society in all its guises, and it is this that allies her with such radical critics of the bourgeois state as Adorno and Marcuse. One might respond that enchantment is not only an unpolitical concept but antipolitical, even reactionary. Sometimes it is. Not in Murdoch's hands, however, where enchantment and a ruthless clarity about reality coexist, albeit not always comfortably. It is this combination that renders her vision of freedom both more and less than liberal but always a "message to the individual," a term that Murdoch (1992, 378) applies to Adorno's teachings, but which fits even better her own.

What "message to the individual" can my study of freedom offer to its subject objects, the people I talked with? That is the topic of the last two chapters. "Transgression with others," the means by which people might become freer, lacks enchantment, even the enchantment of "freedom with," an experience that takes a little magic. We transgress with others in public so that we might find a little magic in our private lives. It is good, in other words, not to mix magic with politics.

CHAPTER 6
TRANSGRESSION WITH OTHERS

In this and the next chapter, I focus on politics not psychology, even as this distinction is more academic than real. The politics are aimed at mitigating the effects of the borderline experience of freedom, such as the tendency to see freedom in the language of all or nothing as well as the tendency to see others as barriers to my freedom, even (or especially) if some of these others are barriers I cannot live without. While I refer frequently to borderline thinking about freedom when proposing the politics I call "transgression with others," the reader should understand that this and the next chapter have an agenda that is different from the previous five chapters: not to characterize the problem but to suggest how to solve it. In fact, there is no solution, only ways of living and thinking that make the borderline experience of freedom less intense.

Transgression with others teaches that if mastery is real, it need not be total. Transgression with others teaches that participation with others can enhance my freedom, not just restrict it. Most importantly, transgression with others teaches that freedom stands in a complex relationship with dependency. Freedom is compatible with dependency when we are able to be dependent on others without insistently being reminded of this fact. Winnicott refers to the ideal relationship between freedom and dependence in terms of the ability to share an illusion similar to the one I called "freedom with." That seems about right. Ironic is that this illusion is best crafted and supported by seeing clearly, liberated as much as humans can be from narcissism, convention, and obsessive attachment. Ironic, in other words, is that we must acknowledge our dependence in order to be free with others.

My approach is informed but not determined by the people I spoke with. Not what is the essence of freedom, and not even what is the best way to think about freedom, but what way of thinking about freedom would be most helpful to informants is the theme of this chapter. Because I am a political scientist, I cannot help thinking that freedom has something important to do with politics. It does, but not the politics that we read about in the newspaper or see on television. The way of thinking about freedom and politics that would be most helpful to people is what I call "transgression with others."

Transgression with others may be defined by characterizing its counterpart, the fully involved and committed Athenian citizen whom John Stuart Mill praises as wiser and more informed than the men of his own time, about 1859, the date *On Liberty* was published.

> It is not sufficiently considered how little there is in most men's ordinary life to give any largeness either to their conceptions or to their sentiments . . . Giving him something to do for the public supplies, in a measure, all these deficiencies. If circumstances allow the amount of public duty assigned to him to be considerable, it makes him an educated man. Notwithstanding the defects of the social system and moral ideas of antiquity, the practice of the diecastery [large citizen juries] and ecclesia [assembly] raised the intellectual standard of an average Athenian citizen far beyond anything of which there is yet an example in any other mass of men, ancient or modern . . . He is called upon, while so engaged, to weigh interests not his own; to be guided, in case of conflicting claims, by another rule than his private partialities. (Mill, quoted in Finley, 1967, 31–32)

The citizen comes from a private realm in which his or her own interest is the paramount reality, in which compromise is unnecessary, the interest of others merely obstacles to his or her will. Working with others draws the private citizen into a common world, tempering not just his or her narcissism but that aspect of conventional wisdom that regards government as incapable of doing anything right unless it does right by me right now. Much contemporary conventional wisdom denies how dependent we are on each other, emphasizing a superficial individualism that is intentionally ignorant of how much we owe to others. Participating with others renders them more real, our dependence upon them both more actual and less narcissistically humiliating, because it is mutual, a shared practice. In other words, participation modulates the tendency toward borderline thinking that seems inherent in the experience of freedom. Though he does not use the language of the borderline, Michael Sandel's praise of republican freedom is based on a similar way of thinking.

My way of thinking about participation is a little different. While I share the views of Mill and Sandel regarding what participation teaches, I see participation as akin to Plato's *techné*, the model for Iris Murdoch's view that skills such as learning a foreign language open us to reality by suppressing the ego. Participation is not necessarily a good in itself. Rather, through participation we learn a skill that is difficult to learn in any other way. Through participation our eyes are opened to a world of others with needs like our own, and unlike our own too. We learn, in other words, how much we live in a world of others whose fates are bound to our own. Through participation one learns that one is not one's own little *autokratôr*, one's own little polis, but a part of the main. Why the participation called transgression with others is the participation best suited to the people I talked with is the focus of this chapter.

Transgression with others is the practice of small-scale politics. It is the opposite of what the political theorist Sheldon Wolin calls "the political," a lofty term explained later. Nor does transgression with others have much to do with those forms of association called civil society, though this has more to do with the way in which the dialog over civil society is currently conducted than with the nature of the concept. Transgression with others understands that freedom in this world (the Western democracies) at this time is best achieved by small-scale insurrection. As the good guerilla never steals from the people among whom he or she is living and fighting, so transgression with others respects the fertile land of constitutionalism, and the freedoms it guarantees.

This claim rests on at least three assumptions:

(a) Participation in politics is not a great good in itself; participation is a means not an end. Above all, participation is a means toward the education of participants.

(b) Ordinary politics is a realm of power and money closed to most people, who lack either the means or the will to participate in the politics of parties and organized interests. Often they lack both.

(c) The real power that makes people crazy is not the power of politicians but the power of experts and bureaucrats.

If the reader sharply disagrees with any of these assumptions, I cannot set him or her straight in this chapter or the next. All I can do is argue that these three assumptions come closest to how the enlightened informant would see his or her world. While the term "enlightened informant" may sound vague, it gains content when one reads the term as stating, "this is how the average person would see things if he or she could see clearly, liberated from the claims of narcissism and convention." Enlightenment means seeing clearly.

The trouble with "transgression with others" is that transgression has become a trendy term. Still it has its advantages, one of which is that transgression can be social as well as political, about something as small as calling a medical doctor by his or her first name when the doctor addresses an older patient by his or her given name. Perhaps the best way to think about transgression with others is in terms of what Michel Foucault calls critique, which might just as well be called the experimental method applied to freedom.

> This critique will separate out, from the contingency that has made us what we are, the possibility of no longer being, doing, or thinking what we are, do, or think. It [this critique] . . . is seeking to give new impetus, as far and wide as possible, to the undefined work of freedom . . . This historical-critical attitude must also be an experimental one. (Foucault, 1984, 46)

Those familiar with Foucault will know that he believed this critique is best practiced locally, not globally, by what he calls local intellectuals (1984, 46). I argue that this critique, understood as "transgression with others," can also be practiced by everyday people like those I spoke with. One reason is because I am writing about freedom not enlightenment. As I have argued, there is a terrible tendency to confuse the two, generally in order to convince us that whatever constrains us is really self-chosen, and thus a mark of our freedom. Foucault's virtue is that he refuses to play this game, instead transforming enlightenment into an experiment with ourselves and others. While Foucault's move represents progress, I will continue to emphasize the difference between freedom and enlightenment. When one does so, the position of local intellectual is open to almost anyone, at least as far as practicing freedom is concerned.

The astute reader will have already noticed the vast disproportion between my analysis of the problem of freedom and my solution, even if the details of transgression with others have not yet been filled in. The problem of freedom, I have argued, rests in the way an evidently natural tendency to divide the experience of freedom in two is worsened by the political economy and ideology of the Western democracies. The solution is small-scale acts of transgression, hardly enough to transform the societies we live in. About this disproportion I can do no better than to recall Adorno's (1974, 57) *frappant mot*, "the almost insoluble task is to let neither the power of others, nor our own powerlessness, stupefy us." Not for a moment do I believe that "transgression with others" will change the society, culture, and politics that reinforce the borderline experience of freedom. What it might do is prevent a few more of us from becoming stupefied by the power of the given. Sometimes that is the best one can do, at least for now. Recall that Simone Weil made almost an identical point. "Only he who knows the empire of might and knows how not to respect it is capable of love and justice" (Weil, 1977a, 181). Transgression with others is one way of not respecting the empire of might.

Civil Society

Civil society is a hot topic these days among social theorists. The university where I teach has recently received millions of dollars in grants to study the topic. My study has benefited from a few thousands of these dollars. The term "civil society" generally refers to all those nongovernmental organizations that bring citizens together, from the Elks Club to the PTA. One might even include the corner bar, celebrated in the old television series "Cheers," as part of civil society. Civil society is a school for responsible citizenship. Even bowling leagues count as part of civil society, which is where Robert Putnam (2000) got the title for his book on the decline of civil society, *Bowling Alone*. Almost as many Americans bowl as they ever did, but they bowl alone or with small groups of friends, not in teams that play in leagues. Or so Putnam tells us. Bowling alone has become a metaphor for the decline of civil society.

Those who write about civil society are not primarily concerned with freedom, even if a vision of positive freedom, the freedom that stems from participation with others in one's own governance, is hovering in the background. Many who write about civil society are concerned with social trust and social capital. One wonders what the young people I interviewed would say to them. Probably they would say that social trust and social capital have little to do with their freedom, and even less with their lives. These young people could be wrong, of course, but even Alexis de Tocqueville might agree with them. Aspects of Tocqueville's vision of freedom come closer to addressing their concerns.

Tocqueville came to the United States in 1831, ostensibly to study our system of prisons. In fact, he came to study why democracy was compatible with a stable political order in the United States but not in France. In *Democracy in America*, Tocqueville argues that the many civil associations in America are a vast training school for democracy. The only remedy for the excesses of democracy is more democracy, understood as widespread political participation of the type John Stuart Mill idealizes, the participation that produces responsible citizens. One can see why fans of civil society would be so taken with Tocqueville.

It is, of course, a particular Tocqueville (by which I mean a particular interpretation of Tocqueville) that partisans of civil society embrace, Tocqueville as a theorist of social trust and social capital. With the term "social capital," the author of *Bowling Alone* refers to generalized reciprocity, our willingness to trust others. Economists, says Putnam, "have demonstrated how social capital translates into financial capital and resource wealth for business and self-governing units" (288). Tom Tyler (1998, 290) concurs, writing that "governments benefit from receiving the willing compliance of their citizens. Such willing compliance is encouraged by trust."

When Putnam and Tyler write about trust and compliance, they have left the realm of freedom far behind. Not just the realm of negative freedom but positive freedom as well. If positive freedom refers to the freedom to participate in one's self-governance, then they are not even talking about positive freedom. When I bowl with others I become more social, which means I trust the government and my fellow citizens more. That might be good but it's not freedom. Could this trust translate into freedom, as I allow myself to be with others in a less anxious, more relaxed way? Perhaps, but freedom is not a feel good substitute for participation in power, which is why I have been cautious about translating "freedom with" into a political program.

Trust is not one of the contributions of association according to Tocqueville. Nor is social capital, the generalized availability of citizens for social and governmental purposes. For Tocqueville, association serves three purposes:

(a) standing resistance to government;
(b) a substitute for government;
(c) release and relief from private life.

The first two purposes see association as an alternative locus of power, a source of power not formed and framed by governmental institutions and purposes.[1] Though Putnam is sometimes regarded as a contemporary version of Tocqueville, the first two senses of association are largely absent in Putnam's work. Only the third contribution of association mentioned by Tocqueville finds much place in Putnam's account, civil society as an antidote to anomie, the normlessness that afflicts modern societies. Some who write of civil society come closer to Tocqueville's vision, such as Theda Skocpol (1999), who is concerned with how civil associations confront and use political power. Nevertheless, it is not the similarity but the difference between Tocqueville's vision and that of many contemporary advocates of civil society that is striking.

To be sure, Tocqueville hopes that participation will create a larger, more social man or woman, one who knows that he must harmonize his interests with others in order to get anything done. "As soon as a man begins to treat of public affairs in public life, he begins to perceive that he is not so independent of his fellow-men as he had at first imagined, and that, in order to obtain their support, he must often lend them his cooperation" (2000, 485–488). But, it would be a mistake to read this simply, or even primarily, as a lesson in social trust. It is a lesson in the "art of being free," as Tocqueville (2000, 229) puts it.

The art of being free is the art of using association for political purposes. Not for purposes of good feeling and belonging but for getting what one wants. Tocqueville's attitude toward the art of association is much like his attitude toward religion. It will not transform human nature. People will still want what is best for themselves, mostly more money (Tocqueville, 2000, 417–424). But in conjunction with others, people are likely to pursue their self-interest both more honestly and more efficiently. The doctrine of self-interest well understood Tocqueville calls it, and that seems about right.[2]

Most young people do not have a clue about self-interest well understood, and it is this that is lacking in their accounts of freedom and in their lives. It is this that explains their bafflement. They were promised freedom and find themselves in a world of constraints and limits. They don't need more social trust; they wouldn't know what to do with it if they had it. If somehow they could be convinced of the virtues of social trust, they would have fallen into false-consciousness. If, that is, we define true-consciousness as how the individual would likely see his or her situation if he or she could see it a little more clearly. This is not the most precise standard around, but it provides some guidance, especially if we define seeing clearly as Murdoch does: insight free of the illusions of narcissism and convention.

Young people believe what Carel the mad cleric believes: that force and fate rule the world. Indeed, young people add an interesting twist (discussed in chapter 2): who possesses power is itself a matter of fate not a matter of right, so it might as well be they. Why people believe this is not clear, but it seems to be a consequence of what Tocqueville (2000, 3) called the equality of condition. By this term Tocqueville meant not literal equality but the loss of fundamental distinctions among people, especially distinctions based upon class, profession, or family. This loss is the leading characteristic of the modern world, one that struck Tocqueville with fear and wonder, a type of religious terror he called it. Today most of us welcome the loss of many of the distinctions associated with the old regime. But, when taken to an extreme, equality must make every distinction arbitrary. This does not, as it turns out, lead to the loss of distinction— that is, to equality. On the contrary, it leads to the loss of meaning associated with distinction, quite a different matter.

Not only is it mere fate that you are rich and I am poor but everything you have, including your talents, abilities, and virtues, might as well have been mine. In what is arguably the most influential work in political theory written in the twentieth century, *A Theory of Justice*, the late John Rawls (1971) argues that a just society would be one in which citizens agreed to the structure of class differences without knowledge of what their own position in the class hierarchy would be. Rawls calls this assumption the veil of ignorance. Because the distribution of innate or natural talents is arbitrary from a moral point of view, their fruits should be shared so as to benefit the least advantaged. The veil of ignorance is designed to guarantee that this is what people choose, for they choose knowing they could end up on the bottom of the social heap, the foot of the avalanche as Lloyd put it.

Rawls's assumptions would not be alien to most young people, who regard power and wealth as matters of fate. Alien is only Rawls's conclusion that because they are morally arbitrary, the fruits of my talents and abilities should be shared. No, precisely because the division of talents and resources is morally arbitrary, I get to keep what I've got and so do you. That's what arbitrary means. As relativism is a poor argument for tolerance, so arbitrariness is a poor argument for sharing, or even for justice.[3] This, at least, is how I believe that most people I talked with would respond to Rawls.

Transgression with others refers to the idea inspired by Tocqueville, but hardly his alone, that others are often the best teacher about one's self-interest. It is through acts of transgression with others that individuals are most likely to understand their freedom's often unwitting dependence on others. This is what Tocqueville means by self-interest well understood. Isn't this what Putnam and Tyler are talking about? No. They put social trust first. Trusting citizens are a resource for public purposes. I put mastery first, arguing that the world being what it is, most people will find that mastery is most readily achieved in conjunction with others.

Although Tocqueville (2000, 482) does not admire individualism, he does not regard it as a moral failing, such as egoism (*égoïsme*) or selfishness would be. Individualism has more the quality of an intellectual error, and in this regard is akin to what the ancient Greeks called *hamartia*, a term that is often translated as the "tragic flaw" that marks a tragic hero. In fact, *hamartia*, which means literally to miss the mark or make a mistake, had nothing to do with a tragic flaw of character (Aristotle, *Poetics*, c 13). That interpretation is a Renaissance invention. *Hamartia* is simply an intellectual mistake, an error in judgment, generally about one's own interests. This is how I am approaching the individualism of informants. Conversely, "transgression with others" is not designed with the moral improvement of informants in mind. It is designed simply to make them smarter about their own interests.

Transgression with Others Is the "Art of Being Free"

Transgression with others is not freedom. Transgression with others is the political activity most likely to allow us to see reality clearly, above all to see how much we depend on others for our freedom. In this way, transgression with others mitigates the borderline tendencies that seem almost inherent in the experience of freedom, but are in any case aggravated by the way most of us live in the United States today.

Transgression with others is distinguished from two other political activities. First, it is distinct from the associations of civil society, at least as these are talked about by Putnam, Tyler, and others. These associations frequently fail to address power. Second, transgression with others is distinguished from more conventional political activities, such as political organizing, lobbying, fund-raising, and running for office. These conventional political activities may be more effective, or less, than transgression with others. They address power but they are the activities of politicos, those already involved in the system. It is hard to imagine more than one or two of the people I talked with being drawn to them.

The type of power that people are more concerned with is what Michel Foucault calls disciplinary power: not an act of Congress but an act of one's HMO. Disciplinary power is the power wielded by experts by virtue of their knowledge, such as the power of one's doctor to deny a referral to a specialist on the grounds that "this is a straightforward medical problem that any internist can treat," as Dave put it quoting his wife's doctor. Of course, disciplinary power and political power are related, and it is good to know this. Congress sets the rules under which HMO's act. But this doesn't mean that writing your congressman or campaigning for her opponent is the path to freedom or mastery. The political regime under which we live is sclerotic, deeply influenced by private power and money and relatively inaccessible to ordinary citizens.

There are exceptions. Mothers against Drunk Driving (MADD), founded by Candy Lightner, has been effective, though one might argue that MADD comes closer to transgression with others, at least in its younger days. Lightner has long since been kicked off the board of MADD for her "impulsive administrative style," as MADD puts it on their website (www.madd.org/news). MADD now receives a large portion of its funding from the automobile insurance industry (Weed, 1993).

One might argue, along lines laid down by Sartre (2003), that MADD was transformed from a practice of freedom into the practico-inert, his term for almost any institution. This is true, however, only if one believes that groups like MADD, or ACT UP (an AIDS activist group which combines direct action with sophisticated lobbying), were once spontaneous practices of freedom rather than sites where individuals may learn about and practice transgression with others. If these groups are the latter, then there is no spontaneous practice of freedom to be lost, even as the sclerotic group becomes less able to teach important lessons about freedom. In other words, groups may facilitate freedom but only individuals are free. Nothing in the concept of "freedom with" contradicts this conclusion.

Transgression with others is what Tocqueville's civic associations should look like today. If, that is, we are concerned with what Tocqueville was concerned with: not social capital and social trust but the cultivation of the art of being free, what Tocqueville calls self-interest well understood. Self-interest well understood is missing from people's lives for two reasons. The first reason is the most common and obvious. Most people lack an education in the benefits of alliance and they lack experiences in the art of association.

The second reason is more subtle and disturbing. Tocqueville (2000, 490) wrote that associations take the place of powerful private persons whom the equality of conditions has eliminated. Think of what this means: becoming politically aware means becoming aware of one's powerlessness as an individual. For some this is an almost unbearable narcissistic injury, an injury to one's pride and self-esteem. Or, as Jason puts it, "my homeowner's association said I couldn't put up a shed in my own backyard. I think that's totalitarian."

Did you ever think of joining the homeowner's association or running for office, I replied?

"I went to a homeowner's meeting once. I couldn't stand it, and went home early. When you're in a group like that, especially one that can tell you what to do, you're nothing. So I went for a drive. That made me feel better."

How many commercials for cars are aimed at people like Jason, who feel nothing so much as humiliated by their associations with others, at least their political associations? Tocqueville says that the alternative to association is the despotism of the state. To this we should add consumerism. Here is a case in which both narcissism and conventionalism (consumerism is both) prevent Jason from seeing his situation more clearly.

Jason is not the norm but he is hardly the exception. Lumara is an exception, an American born in Baltimore of recent African descent.

A member of her extended family in the United States has cancer and needs a bone marrow transplant. Her family members are eager to donate, but those who match most closely are prevented from doing so by a government policy that forbids recent immigrants from certain African countries from donating bone marrow, due to fear of contamination with the AIDS virus. The ill family member is willing to take the risk. The marrow will go to no one else but the appropriate agencies won't say yes.[4]

After much family discussion, the family has turned to other African families in the area, and together they have launched a lobbying campaign designed to change the position of the hospital and government agencies. Not just letters but group "visits" to the director of the hospital, which evidently involve the virtual occupation of his waiting room for several hours, coupled with interviews with the local media, are on their agenda.

One might look at Lumara's story in two ways. One might argue that while her family is practicing the art of association, their motives remain fundamentally selfish. Their perspectives are not enlarged and rendered more social, except perhaps in the limited sense that the extended family feels closer in the face of a hostile government. They just want to help one of their own. Conversely, one might argue that they are creating social trust, joining an immigrant family to the larger "family" of the United States, as they learn to use the tools and resources of democracy.

Nancy Rosenblum (1998, 41), author of *Membership and Morals*, is concerned that many civic associations lead citizens away from a concern with the common good and toward the good of their own group. In other words, groups can be at least as selfish as individuals. About Lumara's "association," Rosenblum says that it doesn't really count as a civic association.[5] The activities of Lumara's extended family are too transitory, informal, and private, even if they came to involve other members of the African American community in their struggle. Rosenblum is probably right as far as the taxonomy of association is concerned, but it doesn't matter. We must come to terms with temporary associations like Lumara's if we are to foster freedom in the United States today, for it is in these temporary associations that transgression is combined with social creativity. Compare Lumara's story with Mark Reinhardt's (1997, 166–178) discussion, in *The Art of Being Free*, of the activities of ACT UP. Reinhardt is aware that an AIDS activist group is not the most likely instance of "the political," concerned as it is with something as private and personal as an illness of the body. What makes Reinhardt think ACT UP has something to do with "the political" is the way ACT UP creates a public space where none existed, albeit one that little resembles traditional public spaces, being both more transitory and anarchic. As Cindy Patton (1990, 131) states, "AIDS activists know that silence equals death but we also know that this cannot simply be said, it must be performed in an anarchistic politics that sometimes . . . seems simply mad in the traditional public realm."

Against "the political," the political philosopher Hannah Arendt (1998) sets not the private realm of friends and family, but what she calls the social, a concept so nebulous that Hannah Pitkin titles her book about it *The Attack of the Blob: Hannah Arendt's Concept of the Social.* One way to make the social less nebulous is simply to define it: the social is the realm of bureaucracy, administration, and experts, where political power is exercised under the guise of rationality and expertise not will or power. Or as Pitkin (1998, 252) puts it, "the social unmythologized . . . should be understood as the absence of politics where politics belongs." From this perspective, Lumara and her family are practicing politics, bringing what is essentially an act of political protest into the hospital director's office, that sanctum sanctorum of the social.

Developing this vision of politics further, it will be helpful to turn to the most famous French philosopher since Sartre, Michel Foucault, who died in 1984. (No philosopher would have appreciated the activities of ACT UP more than Foucault; not just because he died of AIDS but because its transgressive spirit matches his own.) Though both Arendt and Foucault conclude that bureaucracy and administration are the greatest contemporary threats to freedom, Foucault's analysis would be more helpful to the people I talked with, as it does not idealize politics or publicity.[6] On the contrary, Foucault finds freedom in anonymity. "More than one person, doubtless like me, writes in order to have no face," he says (Miller, 1993, 19).

Fascinating character that he is, I approach Foucault in a simple and straightforward fashion, as the theorist who sees power and politics everywhere and not just in the traditional places—such as legislatures, laws, and courts, but in the judgments of experts of all kinds. At work throughout society is a subtle type of power that Foucault calls discipline, which functions through the diagnosis and treatment of all kinds, including the categories of law and bureaucracy, but above all the categories of science and medicine.

Foucault characterizes the power of discipline in terms of what he calls the gaze (*le regard*). Epitome of the gaze is the Panopticon, Jeremy Bentham's name for the tower from which a guard could watch all the prisoners at once in his imaginary circular prison. Because the observation platform was darkened and shaded, the prisoners never knew if and when anyone was looking and at whom. All they knew is that someone could be watching anyone at anytime (Foucault, 1979).

Foucault's father was a doctor, and that is perhaps the best way to explain his concept of the gaze. The gaze represents the tacit observational principles of the experienced clinician, knowledgeable about individuality and particularity, uninterested in what goes on inside, except as it is manifest as a change in the surface. The gaze represents the way in which experts of all kinds classify citizens and so render them patients: not just of doctors but patients of lawyers, bureaucrats, scientists, teachers, and experts of all kinds. The gaze is the way postmoderns are disciplined.

For a generation of social theorists in the 1970s and 1980s, Foucault's image of the Panopticon and all it represents was the leading image of domination in contemporary society. It is for this reason that "Eye Promise," the software that promises liberation by watching your every move on the Internet, is such a discordant image of freedom, as though never the I but only the Eye could be trusted. Yet, one can learn from almost anyone, and it is interesting to think about why "Eye Promise" might be experienced as liberating. Perhaps not just because it promises relief from the punitive but weak superego, but also because Eye Promise is the simulacrum of "freedom with." Like the Panopticon, like freedom itself, Eye Promise has an illusory quality. Somebody might be watching, but maybe not. Does one's "accountability partner" even read his e-mail? (Eye Promise sends him a daily e-mail update of the websites one has viewed.) Does he care? Do I? Eye Promise creates an illusion akin to "freedom with," albeit one in which the space between us is framed and formed by shame and guilt. Perhaps this is as close as some people get to "freedom with."

We should, continues Foucault, understand power not in terms of "right" but in terms of "technique," not in terms of "law" but in terms of "normalization," by which he means the power to convince people to remain in (or become) socially acceptable categories, such as "wife" or "citizen." It is primarily against this power that transgression is aimed. From Foucault's perspective, the expert is more powerful than the politician, and certainly more insidious, though of course it depends on which expert and which politician. In general, however, experts are more powerful, as their power is expressed as knowledge rather than will— that is, expert power does not even appear as power but as objective knowledge, which any rational person must recognize.

The people I spoke with know all this and more, even if they lack the conceptual categories to put it into a practical, everyday theory that would be helpful to them. All they know is that they have been told they are free but don't feel it. They feel constrained and controlled in most aspects of their lives. All complain; only a few know how to resist very effectively. Lumara's family and ACT UP are resisting this power. Though most people lack the language to talk about freedom in similar terms, their views are only one or two steps removed from this formulation. At least they would understand it. Freedom is not abstract but real, not ideal but material, about what I require to experience not just more choices but feelings of expansiveness and comfort in my world.

Mary puts it this way. "I know I'm free when I can feel relaxed and move around. It doesn't happen very much these days, though. I owe too much money, and have too many obligations. Sometimes at night though, when I come home after everyone is asleep, I stretch out on the carpet. I don't have to present myself to anybody. Then I feel free."

Mary's is not a vision of freedom inspired by Foucault but it is a way of experiencing freedom that might one day be transformed into resistance and transgression, which creates another type of space to stretch out in. Foucault would presumably appreciate the locus of Mary's freedom in her body's need to stretch out in the darkness while feeling unobserved. For Mary, freedom is not an intellectual ideal but a bodily reality. Something like Mary's experience seems to be what Lumara was refer- ring to when she said, "At first we sat [in the hospital director's waiting room] like we were patients waiting to see the doctor. I even read his magazines. But soon we spread out all over the place, like it was our liv- ing room."

In this experience, mastery and relaxation were combined, only now we see that it was not the type of mastery that most people seek, that of power and money. Rather, Lumara and her family found relaxation in a transgression that, while possibly violating the law, was evidently not deeply threatening to others. To be sure, the equilibrium was fragile. Had the hospital director called the police to remove Lumara and her family, everything would have changed in a moment. Theirs would no longer have been an experience of freedom but of resistance, and perhaps even terror. But a proper (i.e., non-borderline) understanding of freedom reminds us how much our freedom depends on the often tacit indulgence of others. One wishes it wasn't this way. How could freedom depend on others' indulgence? But it does.

How might those concerned with civil society deal with these con- siderations? Consider Robert Wuthnow's (1999) fascinating claim that 75 million Americans are involved in self-help groups, everything from Alcoholics Anonymous to prayer groups to book discussion groups. Those who write about civil society are ambivalent about such groups.

"Does membership fuel narcissism or cooperation?" asks Rosenblum (1998, 8).

What if we thought about politics as Foucault does, as operating in and through a world dominated by experts who exert their power as though it were knowledge. Imagine that in such a world a new self-help group is formed. The purpose of the group is to discuss body image and the cult of thinness, so that the group's members might feel less oppressed by the culture's images of beauty.

A group less politically relevant is hard to imagine, each of its members concerned with his or her body image. Yet, if Foucault is correct, this group is intensely political, its members liberating their embodied psyches (those familiar with Foucault will understand that he would probably put it the other way around, "enpsyched bodies") from the most oppressive and omnipresent power around, the power to classify and evaluate the body on the basis of abstract standards administered by experts, from doctors to the editors of fashion magazines. Such a group would be practicing transgression with others.

Do Wuthnow's self-help groups successfully address the power with which Foucault is concerned? Perhaps the small groups about which Wuthnow writes foster even more effective forms of self-discipline. Possibly it depends on the group. Questions like this are not being asked often enough by those who study civil society, and that is the point. Rosenblum (1998, 363) comes close, concluding that "experience confirms the variable, often unpredictable personal moral significance of membership." Rather than connecting us to government or generating more social trust, association may indulge narcissism or even hatred. Indeed, Rosenblum's (1998, 317) reference to jury nullification invokes a transitory association similar to that idealized by Reinhardt, and practiced by Lumara, even if the institution of the jury functions as a more traditional container within which to transgress—that is, within which to find a space for freedom. Still, Rosenblum's focus is on the "moral uses of pluralism," whereas mine is on the individual exploitation of pluralism for the purposes of freedom. It's not quite the same thing.

If Rosenblum comes close to understanding how associations may serve individual freedom, Putnam does not, and not because he assumes, contra Foucault, that all power is sovereign. Putnam knows well that power stems from the bottom up, which is why he wants to make more of it available for social and governmental purposes. To be sure, the bottom is not the same thing as Foucault's margin but they are not entirely different categories either. Both recognize that power is dispersed among its subject objects. The difference is that a follower of Foucault would not assume that the power available to citizens through self-help groups would or should be made available for social and governmental purposes. Whether social capital is good depends upon who owns it. One might well argue that it should remain dispersed in the hands of its 75 million small owners. At least they should have more say in how their power is used by others.

Free Association

More often than not, the civil society debate has put Tocqueville's point backward, as though the goal was generalized social trust. No, the goal is for citizens to participate more fully in the political decisions that affect their lives, and so come just a little bit closer to the freedom about which Cicero and Ralph Nader write, freedom as participation in power. Every other form of participation, while enjoyable and valuable, has the quality of a hobby, like bowling: personally enriching perhaps but not the stuff of politics. Only participation in power fulfills people's desire for mastery over their own lives. With this desire there is nothing wrong. Wrong (or rather, ignorant of their dependence on others) is how many would realize this mastery as an individual project.

Political participation means participation in making the decisions that affect one's life. This assertion comes from the Port Huron statement of the Students for a Democratic Society (SDS), 1962, a document of another era, now light years away. The SDS was an offshoot of the League for Industrial Democracy, whose origins date to the turn of the century. It is really this institutional history of the statement that is most interesting: its refusal to confine participation to civic associations; its tendency to see participation as an utterly radical idea, hardly compatible with existing institutions. This is the irony of the views of freedom of so many young people. Though they do not know it, they are making a radical demand. They do not know it because they see no possible connection between how they define freedom, how they experience it, and how it might be institutionalized. What they want is individual power. What they could possibly get is participation in power.

Several years ago, I interviewed a number of former South Korean dissidents (Alford, 1999). Most were depressed. As young men and women they had brought about the downfall of the dictators, and now they live in a world without historical alternatives. Busy starving its people, North Korea is no longer a model of liberation, and since the fall of the Berlin Wall it appears as though no alternative to global capitalism remains. Because they never hoped as much, the mostly young Americans

I talked with are unlikely to become as depressed, but the similarity between these disparate groups is striking. Both live in a world in which historical alternatives have been exhausted, or so it seems to them.

One former dissident was interviewed again, this time about freedom. This is what Song Mien said.

> Several years ago I was asked to write a short story about the 1987 student demonstrations, about what I did and what I felt. Somewhere there I wrote that lying down on the raining street of Chongro [a main thoroughfare] with hundreds of other students shouting "we want democracy," confronting the fierce riot police coming to tear us apart. I felt free for the first time in my twenty years of life. I shed tears not because of the falling raindrops, not because of the tear gas, not because of the fear of arrest and torture, but because of the joy of freedom. It may sound like romanticizing the 1980s but that is what I felt and what I still feel about freedom. By any standard Korea is much freer than in the 1980s. And I now live in very free America. I am free to do anything but I don't feel the joy of being free.

How does one take this statement? As a statement about the limits of American and Korean freedom or about the limits of the experience of freedom per se? Is Song Mien's statement an ideology critique or a gloss on Fichte's bon mot, "to be free is nothing; to become free is heavenly"? Both, but the focus here is on Song Mien's story as an observation about the nature of freedom.

Peak experiences of freedom often have the quality of transgression, of crossing a previously forbidden boundary, of suddenly and explosively expanding one's world. This experience of freedom resembles the happiness that Freud (1961, 25) defines as the sudden satisfaction of needs that have been dammed up to a high degree. It is the release that satisfies, the release that is equated with the experience of freedom. One does not want to say that the release is confused with the experience of freedom, for release is a legitimate dimension of the experience of freedom, but only one dimension.

If the problem of freedom is the problem of living between losing and fusing, then the experience of freedom as transgression is an experience confined to the pole of losing, rupturing the bonds of constraint and so liberating oneself to . . . what? To answer this question (which is another way of finding freedom in living everyday life) requires that we see transgression with others not primarily as a liberating moment but as a practice through which we learn about how much our freedom depends on others, a much more sobering lesson.

Consider Danielle, a French Canadian who became an American citizen. Several years ago she converted to Islam. She talks as though it were a strictly intellectual decision; Islam, the one religion that allows her to worship all the great monotheistic prophets, as she calls them. (I suspect it had something to do with her marriage to a man with a Middle Eastern name, but love and freedom have long made captivating bedfellows.) But, she goes on to say, she would never have converted had she not lived in the United States. Here she has cultural freedom, and the freedom of women's rights, which she would lack in many Islamic countries, and she can't imagine giving that up. She needs both Islam and American law in order to be free.

"I'd been thinking about it for months, and one morning I woke up and knew that today was the day I would become a Muslim. My mother wouldn't speak to me for years. I had to go to court and sue her to get her off my case. But we're reconciled now. That is my experience of freedom."

Would you be as free if you were still alienated from your mother? I asked.

"No, that completes my freedom. It makes everything natural again."

Becoming a Muslim was an act of transgression, an act of freedom. But it took the stability of American law and custom to make it real, as though she had transgressed a boundary but needed law and custom to keep the freedom she had gained from being crushed on the other side. (By "custom" Danielle means something like women's rights and religious tolerance. At the same time, she is troubled by the "custom" of many Americans of seeing Islam as a religion of fanatics.) Her freedom was completed when her relationship with her mother was restored, as though nature must combine with transgression and custom to perfect freedom; as though freedom were a mixture of association, trust, and transgression.

Would it make sense to argue that Danielle is participating in an association that will never be written about in any book on association and civil society, an association that secures her freedom by triangulation, so to speak, somewhere in that space created by Islam, the Constitution of the United States, and her mother? If one were merely recording her formal associations, she would be a Muslim. But her inner associational life is far more complicated, a complex triangulation of transgressions, accommodations, and belongings.

One might argue that it is not the job of political theory to deal with the inner lives of citizens, at least not in the unique and idiosyncratic inner lives of people like Danielle. Perhaps that is so, but the advantage of looking closely at how people use associations is that it reminds us that associations don't exist to create trusting citizens. Associations exist to help their members become more fully developed and diverse human beings. That this individual achievement is not in conflict with association, but requires it, is an observation common to both Mill and Tocqueville. In Mill's famous words, "in proportion to the development of his individuality, each person becomes more valuable to himself, and is therefore capable of being more valuable to others. There is a greater fullness of life about his own existence, and when there is more life in the units there is more in the mass which is composed of them" (Mill, 1975, 59–60).

What needs more emphasis is that this often means individuals will use associations in ways that are not necessarily civil but private, more about transgression than trust. Or rather, even our private pursuits are unavoidably public (and vice versa). George Kateb (1992, 226) quotes Robert Frost to make the same point. "People work together 'whether they work together or apart.' "[7] Transgression with others teaches this lesson.

If Reinhardt overemphasizes the chaos of the art of being free, his instincts are sound. Too much of the civil society debate is concerned with the amelioration of anomie, so that more social capital will be available for government and society. The same may be said about the positive version of this debate, civil society as the opportunity for *Bildung* (self-cultivation), which fosters *Mündigkeit* (mature autonomy), Kant's favorite virtue. Anomie is bad and Mündigkeit is good, but neither of these continental terms is to the point.

One suspects that the love affair with social trust has something to do with allowing those who write about it to avoid really tough questions of politics and power. If "the social unmythologized . . . should be understood as the absence of politics where politics belongs," as Pitkin puts it in explaining Arendt's concept of the social, then one must ask whether some who write about civil society do so because it's easier than writing about politics—that is, about who gets to participate in power.

Talking with people about freedom reminds us that freedom is real, and elusive, about how I live my life every day. Many people understand that their freedom requires power, they just don't know how to get it, except by participating in a way of life that takes as much freedom as it gives, "the economic rat race," as one called it. A few, such as Lumara and Danielle, have taught themselves a more idiosyncratic lesson about freedom and association. Could we learn from them?

CHAPTER 7

ARISTOCRATS OF FREEDOM

Political theorists often write about "the political," as though it were elevated, more than mere politics. The eminent political theorist Sheldon Wolin, defines "the political" as

> an expression of the idea that a free society composed of diversities can nonetheless enjoy moments of commonality when, through public deliberations, collective power is used to promote or protect the well-being of the collective . . . In contrast [to politics], the political is episodic, rare. (Wolin, 1996, 31)

Along with the people I talked with, have I abandoned the political forever? Does transgression with others imitate "the political" on a smaller scale, or merely mock it?

In his recent book, *Tocqueville Between Two Worlds*, Wolin (2001, 264–265) elaborates, characterizing "the political" in terms of what might be called republican socialism (my term), in which popular participation in politics is extended to the realm of economics, but always with politics in the lead. The result is socialism with the emphasis on the term social, understood as public discussion, debate, and sociability. In other words, the political does not stop at the borders of what is called economics as it does under liberalism. Nor does economics drive the political as it does under socialism. Instead, everything that people do is drawn under the umbrella of public discourse and determination. Think of Wolin as a Hannah Arendt of the Left, and you will not be far wrong.

Informants and I have abandoned this ideal. Informants do so for the most part unknowingly, and hence without regret. The political was never there for them to miss or lose, not even as an ideal. For all the sometimes subtle differences between younger and older people, they are agreed that American freedom means the freedom to get an education and make money.

I abandon Wolin's ideal knowingly, and with some regret. My regret is lessened when I listen to people like Bob, 45 years old, who first defines freedom as making peace with a difficult coworker and then talks about quitting his job, putting his furniture into storage, and going to Kansas for three months in order to research its territorial history, with which he became fascinated. There he spent his days in the library and his evenings playing tennis and drinking beer. He was, he says, inspired by the first history course he took when he returned to college at 40. Bob's goal is to become a historian. He made good money running his own business but it wasn't satisfying.

The question that motivates Tocqueville and Wolin is whether freedom is possible in the modern world. Looking at people like Bob, one has to answer yes. Bob is a free man. Bob does not, it seems, practice the transgression of disciplinary boundaries. Instead, he transgresses the boundaries of convention—of what is expected at various stages of life. While Bob transgresses these boundaries alone, at this point in his life he does not need others to show him the way. Bob is the man who has already defined freedom as getting along with others. Bob is the aristocrat whom Tocqueville so admired, the one who escapes the leveling equality of condition and brings something new and different to the world, even if it is just the example of his life. Dressed in shorts and a T-shirt, Bob doesn't look or act like an aristocrat, but he is. So are Lumara and Danielle.

"Aristocratic" freedom is seeing clearly while living as creatively as possible, liberated from the constraints of narcissism, convention, and obsessive attachment. It is ironic that while aristocratic freedom is a strictly individual achievement, it generally depends on the company of others. Transgression with others is not the only form this company takes, but it is one especially suited to young people and the world they live in. Aristocratic freedom takes money but not much, and in the Western democracies we live in wealthy societies with a large social surplus. Above all, aristocratic freedom requires the capacity to bring imagination and reality into mutual contact. In other words, aristocratic freedom requires the power of illusion, the mark of "freedom with."

Wolin dismisses Tocqueville's vision of aristocratic freedom, arguing that for its sake he sacrifices the political. The early Tocqueville, says Wolin, is the theorist of a mundane, interest-based politics that at its best enlarges the perspectives of its participants. This is the Tocqueville of volume one of *Democracy in America*, the Tocqueville who so admired the New England town meeting. But it is not the mature Tocqueville, the one who became involved in French politics and became disillusioned.

The mature Tocqueville desperately longs for "the political" but cannot bear the threat it poses to order and property, becoming in the end the liberal aristocrat he always was. For this Tocqueville, participation serves primarily to preserve some diversity in a world that is becoming increasingly one-dimensional. Participation, in other words, is not a way of participating in politics but of preserving a modicum of human variety in an increasingly monotonous world. Participation does so by bringing people out of their private worlds into shared endeavors and new perspectives. In this way, participation increases the possibilities for freedom, helping people see themselves and their situations more clearly.

This is the vision of participation I am arguing for. Transgression with others fosters the tendency to see one's situation more clearly. When one does so, one is free in something like the aristocratic sense Tocqueville had in mind, free to live one's life more creatively, less bound by narcissism and convention, as one has joined the world without merging with it.

Does this mean that we transgress with others in order to experience our own uniqueness, that mastery is more personal means than collective end? Yes and no. Transgression with others, unlike league bowling (Putnam's example), or attending a PTA meeting, is an activity that in our disciplined world is likely to achieve results, as it works in those social spaces vulnerable to organized intervention—that is, to politics. It is neither coincidence nor foregone conclusion that it is this same activity that is likely to foster uniqueness. That is just the way it works right now in a world that combines highly centralized and virtually impregnable political power with decentralized but pervasive *pouvoir social*, as Tocqueville calls it, similar to what Foucault calls discipline. There is no guarantee that 50 years ago, or 50 years hence, this was or will remain the case. Transgression with others is a strategy for freedom for a large but hardly universal class. But perhaps the days of a universal class are gone forever.

For Tocqueville, the relative equality of condition meant the rise of a new form of power separated from its sovereign sources, operating not through coercion but through conviction of its subject objects. Social power is dispersed so that it cannot be assembled and used as kings once drew upon their power. *Pouvoir social* exists in the minds and *moeurs* of citizens, in the way in which they identify with each other. This power, says Tocqueville, covers the surface of society

> with a network of small, complicated, painstaking, uniform rules through which the most original minds and the most vigorous souls cannot clear a way to surpass the crowd; it does not break wills, but it softens them, bends them, and directs them . . . it does not destroy, it prevents things from being born . . . I have always believed that this sort of regulated, peaceful servitude, whose picture I have just painted, could be combined

better than one imagines with some of the external forms of freedom, and it would not be impossible for it to be established in the very shadow of the sovereignty of the people. (Tocqueville, 2000, 663–664)

This is not yet Foucault. Tocqueville is talking about a diffuse quality of mind, the result of the loss of distinctions associated with equality. Foucault is talking about what he calls capillary power that infiltrates from definite loci on the margins of society, such as prisons and clinics. Perfected on the margins of society, disciplinary power slowly migrates to the center of society, where it becomes a model for all power based upon knowledge and expertise, such as the power of lawyers, doctors, teachers, and bureaucrats.

Especially in the second volume of *Democracy in America*, Tocqueville (2000, 485–492) sees association and participation not just (or even primarily) as a way of "affecting policy," as they say today, but as drawing individuals out of the privacy of their own lives, so that they might see, feel, and participate in the diversity of ways of life that Tocqueville equates with freedom—that is, with the legacy of aristocratic variety. Mill's view was similar but less political.

Though his understanding was more practical than theoretical, Tocqueville intuited something important about disciplinary power, the way in which it could be used to depoliticize political protest. Recalling a conversation with a physician who operated an asylum for the insane, Tocqueville says that the doctor confided to him that he had treated several of the revolutionary leaders. About this Tocqueville comments: "I have always thought that in revolutions, especially in democratic revolutions, madmen—not those who are given the name metaphorically, but genuine madmen—have played a very considerable political role." Both the physician and his revolutionary patients, Tocqueville concludes, should be locked up in an asylum. About this episode Wolin opines, "Tocqueville depoliticizes what might seem an important moment by placing the actions beyond the political pale, literally in a context of insanity" (Wolin, 2001, 457).

If Wolin is correct, as I believe he is here, then treating transgression with others as politics means returning to politics those political power relationships that have been mislabeled as apolitical, that is about knowledge not power. To be sure, transgression with others does not create a political realm in Wolin's sense, what he calls "the political." But transgression with others does create a political realm if we mean by this the return of politics to realms of the social from which politics has gone underground.

Why is that not enough, especially given that the goal remains individual freedom, which must in any case be achieved one person at a time?

Wolin (2001, 560) accuses Tocqueville of the aestheticization of politics, characterized by a longing for grandeur of thought and deed. But does not Wolin do the same, wanting if not a beautiful politics certainly a grand one? "The political" is nothing if not grand.

An advantage of interviewing people about freedom is that one is constantly reminded that while freedom is a political concept, it remains an individual achievement, a property of people like Bob, who quit work for a dream of Kansas. Aspects of our culture make it more difficult for most people to achieve freedom, but this does not mean that freedom is a collective achievement and in this sense grand, the triumph of a people. On the contrary, freedom remains a property of individuals not of the people, just people, one by one, a new aristocracy, composed of people such as Bob, Lumara, and Danielle.

Do these free men and women experience freedom in less borderline terms? Yes, though not everyone needs to participate in transgression with others in order to overcome borderline tendencies in their experience of freedom. Several people I spoke with whose views of freedom were not borderline did not practice transgression with others; indeed they did not practice politics period. The world is complicated, with many multiple, overlapping, and even contradictory, explanations. Mine is one, and it is no contradiction to state that while some achieve non-borderline conceptions of freedom on their own, for most, especially young people, transgression with others is invaluable in teaching the lessons they need to learn in order to mitigate their tendency to experience freedom in the language of all or nothing. Since most young people are not borderline in a clinical, diagnostic sense, this is a lesson they are able to learn from experience.

What lesson is this? That the real but limited mastery that people may exert over their own lives has more the quality of a skill of living with others than it does with autarky. Can we put a label on this vision of freedom? Should we? Phenomenal freedom is the view that comes closest. For an exponent of phenomenal freedom, such as Michael Oakeshott (1991), freedom is a skill or talent that is developed over time. Freedom is proficiency in life, a bravura performance at the task of living. Freedom is a miscellany of skills, talents and abilities that match attainment with ambition (Farr, 1998, 252).[1] From this perspective, freedom has the quality of what the ancient Greeks called *arête* or human excellence.

While it would be incorrect to say that this *arête* is located somewhere toward the middle of a continuum between losing and fusing, or mastery and respite, the *arête* of phenomenal freedom requires the ability to see reality clearly, free of the Siren calls of narcissism and convention.[2]

Phenomenal freedom avoids the extremes to which freedom may be pursued and so lost. This includes the extremes of negative and positive freedom, such as believing that I (or people in general) can be free only when mass society is eliminated or corporate capitalism transformed. It is toward this last extreme that intellectuals are particularly vulnerable.

One intellectual not vulnerable to such extremes (or at least he does not succumb) is Richard Flathman (2003) in *Freedom and Its Conditions.* Here Flathman argues that self-discipline, such as that practiced by the Stoics, can prepare people to resist the discipline about which Foucault writes, the discipline of experts. Whether this insight is more Flathman than Foucault, Flathman leaves for the reader to decide, and that seems about right (35). Admirable in any case is Flathman's recognition that the best reason to participate with others to secure my freedom is that still others are participating with each other to take away my freedom and yours. Neither you nor I will stop them on our own (31). This is roughly my argument as well, what Flathman calls "muffled echoes or anticipations of the weak Republican view" (24). I would not go as far.

Flathman includes Foucault among those thinkers reaching back to Plato who have found the distinction between higher and lower selves, better and worse desires, to be liberating (167). If I can master my base desires, then not only will I be free from having someone else do it for me, but I will be in a stronger position to resist the disciplinary state, as I will presumably be better able to recognize its intrusions and temptations. (The choice between superego and superstate, as it has been called; I have called it "meant to do that.") It is hard to disagree about this claim of Flathman's (once again, Flathman suggests that it is perhaps as much his claim as Foucault's). Certainly freedom has an agonal quality. And yet this is not the whole story. To see freedom as a constant conflict among me, myself, and I, or between me and others, is to ignore an entire world of freedom. While part of the self wants to transform itself into a great work of art (169), another part of the self wants simply to be: to be among others without constantly having to ask who's on top? Or who is making whom into what? This dimension of freedom, what I have called "freedom with," is largely absent in Flathman's vision of freedom, as it is absent in Foucault's.

If "freedom with" is largely absent in Flathman's book and yet it lives a powerful underground existence, then one would expect to see the desires expressed by "freedom with" work themselves out in pathological and *outré* forms. Or at least this is what Erich Fromm (1969) and others have taught us about the relationship between freedom and totalitarianism in the 1930s and 1940s. I think this is true, and that we have already seen what these forms look like. Only, they are by now so familiar that they are virtually invisible, like water to a fish. Expressed in words that no informant ever used but which come shockingly close to the musings of at least a dozen, this way of thinking would sound like this. "If I can't have freedom with others, then I will become autokratôr, a measure of my disappointment, my fear, and my rage, transformed into a cynical strategy of self-defense in a world in which freedom means protection from the intrusions of others. Whatever freedom remains to be enjoyed, I shall experience at night, alone, or with friends or family, when for a few hours I can let my guard down before I once again gird myself for the struggle." In other words, this way of thinking about freedom would sound remarkably like that of my informants. Only now we see that this way of thinking is not simply pathological and *outré*. On the contrary, it is in some measure a reasonable response to what is experienced as an overwhelmingly hostile and meaningless milieu, akin to Carel's dark cupboard, where force and fate rule the world. We don't often think of how close cynicism stands to rage, but perhaps we should. Cynicism is the rationalization of rage, another mark of the borderline thinking behind the strategies of survival adopted by so many informants.

Transgression with Others Is Not Rational

Toward another extreme, intellectuals are even more vulnerable: the tendency to equate freedom with reason. The greatest thinker in recent years to succumb to this vulnerability is undoubtedly Jürgen Habermas. A greater rationalist than either of his teachers, Adorno and Marcuse, Habermas (1998, xxxv) argues that subjective freedom, the freedom of the individual, only makes sense when it can be rationally justified to others. Why should I be free? Why should you be free? If one cannot answer this question rationally—that is, by giving good arguments, then one's freedom is neither fully rational nor fully legitimate. This is especially so in a world in which theological argument (perhaps citing John 8:32) is no longer compelling to many, at least in the West.

> This shift in perspective to a "transcendence from within" [i.e., without reference to God] raises the question of whether the specific binding force of norms and values can be grounded in the *subjective freedom* and the practical reason of human beings forsaken by God. (1998, 7, my emphasis)

From the perspective of Habermas, the question is whether transgression with others is irrational. On what grounds do I assert my freedom? On what basis do we transgress the bounds of disciplinary authority? What "binding norms and values" can I invoke, other than my desire to be free? The problem, from Habermas's perspective, is not that "transgression with others" doesn't justify itself, but that it can't, because it's all about action not speech. There is something not so much irrational as a-rational about transgression with others, as this transgression is lacking in speech and reason.

There is some truth to this criticism that I imagine Habermas is making. All along I have assumed that the desire of the young people I spoke with to be free is legitimate, just not mature. Rather than answering Habermas's challenge directly, allow me to turn the argument around, asking if Habermas's attempt to justify subjective freedom is compatible with transgression with others. If not, then we shall have to choose.

Like many before him, Habermas assumes that the problem of philosophical fundamental justification in the absence of God is at the same time a problem of freedom. As Habermas puts it, "legal persons can be autonomous only insofar as they can understand themselves, in their exercise of civic rights, as authors of just those rights which they are supposed to obey as addressees" (1998, 258).

Why? For the same reason that philosophers from Rousseau to Kant to Hegel equate freedom with self-authorship, what I called "meant to do that." So that freedom and reason will coincide, so that my will cannot truly be thwarted by your will, as both are in the end the same Will. In Habermas's case, the goal is to demonstrate that freedom is realized in rational union with others in discourse, by which he means the fair, free, and open discussion of fundamental norms and values.[3]

Habermas characterizes this discussion by the repeated use of the term "democratic will formation" [*demokratische Willensbildung*], a term at which thoughtful readers should cringe. Like freedom, will is a property of individuals. Whatever "will" is exactly, it is not a collective noun or a property of the group. To be sure, Habermas employs the term "democratic will formation" with the best will in the world. Unlike Hegel, Habermas understands that freedom is found not just in joining one's will with others but also in refusing to do so. The ability to step back from any particular agreement is also an implication of rational discourse, even if it is not a moment that plays a very big role in Habermas's hopes and dreams for democracy.

One might be tempted to argue that transgression with others has the quality of a mini discourse, a discourse conducted with acts rather than words, but one aimed at the same end, democratic or discursive will formation.[4] That would be wrong. Transgression with others serves to educate its participants, one by one, about their dependence on others for freedom, but freedom remains an individual achievement, an act of seeing clearly that may lead to the creation of a private (i.e., personal) clearing in which that other dimension of freedom, freedom as respite, is occasionally possible. It is out of such experiences that the "aristocratic" experience of freedom, freedom as creative living, is most likely to emerge.

People do not need to be convinced that their norms and values can be justified in a world from which God has fled. This is a problem of philosophers, one that should not be confused with practical political theory, let alone freedom. People need to better understand the sources of their unfreedom, which is another way of saying that they need to better understand that what Foucault calls discipline is not just an act of power (they know that), but that it can be addressed through a type of small-scale politics called transgression with others.

To be sure, the problem with discipline as people experience it resembles what Habermas characterizes as the incursion of the rationalized values of instrumental reason into the world of everyday life. Young people, especially, could benefit from the clarification of their tradition-bound self-understanding, as Habermas calls it. Indeed, transgression with others aims at an aspect of this understanding, generating through practice an ideology critique that demystifies discipline, showing it to be a more subtle and sophisticated assertion of political power. From this perspective, it is actually Habermas's earlier works, roughly from *Toward a Rational Society* through *Legitimation Crisis*, that are most relevant, dealing as they do with the intrusion of instrumental reason into the world of everyday life. One can read these works as less concerned with philosophical justification, more with what ideology critique in advanced industrial society looks like. Most of those I spoke with could benefit from Habermas's characterization of the way in which science and technology act as ideologies, the subject of a fine early essay of his (Habermas, 1970). The result, however, would not be to discursively form informants' wills, but to allow informants to pursue their individual freedom more effectively by helping them see the world a little more clearly.

For Habermas (1998, 267, 265, note 1), the problem is to legitimate the constitutional state (*Rechtsstaat*) in an era in which arguments invoking either God or natural law can no longer be made without embarrassment. The constitutional state is legitimated through a series of public discourses, most of which evidently take place in the types of associations favored by the exponents of civil society. One evaluates the legitimacy of these discourses, and hence the constitutional state, by how close these discourses come to the general symmetry conditions of the ideal speech situation. All this is a fancy way of saying that "a regulation may claim legitimacy only if all those possibly affected by it could consent to it after participating in rational discourses" (1998, 259).

Transgression with others does not imagine that one is free only if one would have consented to the constitution under the conditions of discourse. Seeing the issue in these terms confuses epistemology with freedom, a venerable confusion that need not be continued. Since the gravest threats to individual freedom (at least in the Western democracies) have little to do with the illegitimacy of the constitution, transgression with others carves out a human space from the world of discipline that surrounds us. In theory, and from time to time in practice, the constitution may actually foster that activity.

Though Habermas seeks something similar, the difference is significant. Habermas's goal is to legitimate the power of the state by connecting it to the discourse of citizens, what those who promote civil society should properly be concerned with. Transgression with others would carve out this space for its own sake, or rather, for the sake of those who might find a little freedom there. I believe this version actually comes closer to Tocqueville. How the constitutional state might serve *this* project is the topic of the next section.

Constitutionalism Frames and Forms
Transgression with Others

Informants and Wolin are both wrong to devalue the framework of freedom, the Constitution, the Bill of Rights, and the tradition of constitutionalism or rule of law of which they are a part. Informants devalue these practices because they protect political freedom not the freedom to do what they want. Wolin devalues these practices because they are the infrastructure of liberal freedom not political freedom—that is, the political. In fact, these practices protect not just liberal freedom but the politics of transgression with others. Though I have promised to pursue the problem of freedom from a perspective that respects the experience of informants, this does not mean (as should be obvious by now) that I share their views. About the "symbolic" aspects of freedom, as many call it, they are quite wrong.

Constitutionalism is usually defined as the limitation of government by a fundamental law that is beyond the reach of individual governments to amend. "Writtenness" and entrenchment are central to the tradition. The former means what it seems to mean. Even the constitution of the United Kingdom, often cited as an example of an unwritten constitution, is written down in many places, such as the Magna Carta (1215) and the English Bill of Rights (1689). Entrenchment refers to the guarantee that the powers that are limited by the constitution are themselves not entitled to relax these limitations on their own. The American president can't decide on his own to run for a third term.

Every nation has a constitution. A majority of states fail to practice constitutionalism. Whether constitutionalism requires such institutional elaborations as the separation of powers is subject to debate. The 1803 Supreme Court decision in *Marbury v. Madison* settled the issue in the United States, and while most nations that practice constitutionalism have a similar arrangement, it does not seem essential (Waluchow, 2001).

When students of constitutionalism talk about a "constitutional convention," they are not referring to a meeting but to what Tocqueville called *moeurs*, "social rules arising with the practices of the political community . . . which impose important, but non-legal, limits on government." An example might be that electors chosen to represent the State of Florida in the American Electoral College must vote for the presidential candidate for whom a plurality of Floridians voted. Constitutional conventions are not, of course, always followed, nor are they readily enforced in the courts.

Constitutionalism is not without its critics. Hobbes held that the idea of limited sovereignty is incoherent. Even if the government is limited, the people cannot bind themselves. They can, however, make it more difficult to act, requiring extraordinary majorities and the like. For our purposes, the most powerful objection against constitutionalism comes from critical legal theory, as it is called, which argues that reliance on constitutions and constitutionalism "only serves to rationalize the purely political decisions by judges pursuing, consciously or not, their own political ideologies . . . Instead of the curbing of arbitrary government power for which the idea of constitutionalism is supposed to stand, we have political suppression disguised in the cloak of false constitutional legitimacy."[5] Since there is no "people" but only different groups and classes with varying interests and power, constitutionalism creates a myth of shared interests that doesn't exist.

Something like the objection of critical legal theory would presumably be Wolin's objection as well. Neither he nor Tocqueville is a great fan of constitutionalism, but for different reasons. Tocqueville's objections are readily addressed by constitutionalism as a convention—that is, a *moeur* or social practice. Wolin's objections are not so readily addressed. On the contrary, Wolin's ideal, republican socialism, is attractive. But it is an ideal without a home, detached not just from regime politics but almost any politics as it is currently practiced anywhere in the world. That matters.

Someday that may change, and it is one task of political theory to keep the memory of lost ideals alive. It is not the task of political theory to forget the present to do so. Under the present circumstances, the best hope for freedom is the practice of constitutionalism, understood as a framework within which transgression with others takes place.

To be sure, transgression with others does not require a stable constitutional order. Nor does freedom. Freedom sometimes flourishes best as resistance to sovereign political power. But when one looks at the way in which transgression with others is practiced, one sees how a stable constitutional order frames and forms a space within which transgression can be experienced as liberating. Consider again Danielle, who converted to Islam only because American law and its Constitutional guarantees protected not just her freedom to do so but also her freedom from doing so—that is, her freedom from interpretations of Islam that she finds abhorrent. Similarly, Lumara and her family did not need constitutionalism in order to occupy the hospital director's office, but the freedom they experienced there came into being because they did not have to worry very much about being jailed (at least not for long) and tortured for their acts. The same goes for ACT UP. One may experience freedom in the face of jail and torture, as Song Mien did on the streets of Seoul. But, since freedom does not require this threat, there is no reason to idealize it.

On the contrary, Judith Shklar's (1989, 29) "Liberalism of Fear" reminds us how destructive of freedom institutionalized cruelty truly is. "Systematic fear is the condition that makes freedom impossible, and it is aroused by the expectation of institutionalized cruelty as by nothing else." Constitutionalism mitigates this fear. Even if one holds that freedom of speech is effete, there is nothing effete about what is called freedom from fear, even if one could put it a little differently. Because constitutionalism isn't freedom but only a condition of freedom, what it achieves is not freedom from fear but a state of being lightly held in which freedom may appear if other conditions are right. There is no reason to assume that this freedom must be experienced in public, or even that this is desirable. All that is necessary is that public order not be so terrifying and repressive that freedom cannot appear at all.

Another advantage of distinguishing between freedom and its conditions is that we avoid the objection implied by Sartre, that constitutionalism risks the reification of freedom, the transformation of pure potential into the practico-inert. Because constitutionalism is not freedom but a state of being lightly held within which (other things being equal) freedom may appear, constitutionalism is not the reification of freedom but a supporting condition of some types of freedom, especially that expressed by transgression with others.[6] Danielle can keep her human rights, Lumara does not have to worry very much about being tortured or disappearing, and ACT UP can continue to act up without its members being shot down in the streets. It's easy to forget how important that is. It is equally easy to forget our indebtedness to others, past and present, who made this possible. To recognize one's indebtedness without allowing one's imagination to become impoverished by debt is part of freedom too.

Upon the Constitution, the Bill of Rights, and the tradition of constitutionalism we are all dependent for our freedom. In the absence of this trinity, many could presumably carve out a new freedom, but that does not cancel our indebtedness. To deny or forget our debts is to assert an autonomy we do not possess, pretending that our freedom is not imbricated in a world of others, including those others who founded our constitutional order. It is in this regard, particularly, that I think informants (as well as some political theorists) are wrong, and I seek not to represent but to correct them.

When I state that I take the perspective of informants, I mean that I take up their interest in freedom, not assuming that everything they want is an instance of false-consciousness. Not for a minute do I think that the people I spoke with understand freedom in a way most useful to themselves and others. That way is what I would teach.

Recall Marcuse's remark that the only nonrepressive use of the term "order" is Baudelaire's poetic vision of order's conjunction with beauty. Marcuse is mistaken. Constitutional order is not necessarily repressive, though it may be. Whether constitutional order is repressive depends not just on the order but how we use it. Used as a frame and form for transgression with others, constitutional freedom may become a version of being lightly held, precisely what freedom requires. Because transgression with others does not appear to challenge the stability of political regimes, it is generally afforded constitutional protection. One should not overrate constitutionalism. Many of the whistleblowers I interviewed for another book (Alford, 2001) were overly confident in their ability to use the law to protect themselves. Generally it didn't, and they paid the price of their livelihoods. But not their lives. That counts too.

Transgression with others turns out to be precisely the type of activity that constitutionalism protects best: challenges to practices of power that are not obviously and intimately connected to the stability of the constitutional order itself. One might argue that this means that transgression with others is a lesser form of politics. Better to argue that it is politics on a smaller scale, the scale on which individuals are most likely to experience freedom.

By freedom, Tocqueville meant (especially in the second volume of *Democracy in America*) ways of democratic living that express something of the variety and style of an aristocratic order. On behalf of the people I interviewed, this is the freedom that I choose. If this sounds arrogant, remember that mine is only an exercise in enlightenment. The people I talked with will live as they choose, or at least not as I choose.

For Wolin, freedom is participation in those grand but ephemeral moments that mark the instauration of political regimes. In other words, Wolin holds to a particularly dramatic vision of positive freedom: not merely is freedom participation in one's own governance but it is participation in those revolutionary transformations from which epic political theories are born. In other words, Wolin's vision comes a little too close to that of an enchanted politics. By contrast, I have looked toward the other end of the scale for freedom, not in great instaurations but in tiny transgressive practices that are not so much engendered as they are simply allowed to be born within the framework that is constitutionalism. Sometimes one should take one's freedom where one finds it.

Richard Rorty (1989, 65) takes a position almost the opposite of Wolin's, arguing in *Contingency, Irony, and Solidarity* that the public realm is properly concerned with lessening cruelty and humiliation. Everything else, including the "Nietzschean–Sartrean–Foucauldian attempt at authenticity and purity" is properly restricted to the private realm, lest we turn the public world into a perpetual French Revolution. By lessening cruelty within social structures, Rorty refers to liberal ideals such as improving the quality of education, protecting freedom of the press, and the like. Trouble is, political power, particularly as it is expressed as disciplinary power, does not respect the division between private and public.

"Transgression with others" refuses to recognize the false boundary between private and public. At the same time, transgression with others avoids the tendency among some intellectuals to "hope for paroxysms where nobody should want them—in politics," as Rorty (1993) once put it. Otherwise expressed, I am making a distinction between big politics and little politics (transgression with others) at roughly the same point where Rorty draws the distinction between public and private. That's a big difference, even if it does not appear so at first glance.

Ever since the seventeenth century, freedom had been defined as all great philosophy's . . . concern. Philosophy had an unexpected mandate from the bourgeoisie to find transparent grounds for freedom. (Adorno, 1987, 214–215)

One might argue that the embrace of constitutionalism and the order that it represents, unwittingly participates in the directive given philosophy by the bourgeoisie. On the contrary, the bourgeois freedoms of constitutionalism (for that is precisely what they are) are frames and forms that may be used by individuals in order to pluck a little bit of freedom from the web of rationalization. That this plucking is generally more effective when individuals work together reminds us not to take the guarantees of constitutionalism too literally, lest we fall victim to the story about the prince, the pauper, and the bridge. (Under the equality of the law, it is illegal for both paupers and princes to sleep out under the bridge at night.) While constitutionalism guarantees individual liberty, it is most effectively practiced as transgression with others.

This argument assumes that it is not governmental power but private power, the power of experts and bureaucrats, which is the greater enemy of freedom. This is what the people I talked with say, and about this they are not mistaken. One might argue that governmental power is so implicated in the pursuit and preservation of private power that one cannot be used against the other. Sometimes this is true and sometimes not. The old (not classical but post New Deal) liberalism was not wrong, just old. In any case, the web of rationalization is not as seamless as all that. To know this is to catch a glimpse of freedom. To use it is to become a little freer.

Transgression with others finds its freedom within the iron cage, as Weber (1958, 181) called the regime of rationalization that marks the modern world. Beginning as an instrumental practice, transgression with others teaches us about our dependence on others without idealizing this dependence as though it itself were freedom, the freedom of passionate commitment that transcends the bounds of reason. For Weber, passionate commitment is one of the few ways out of the iron cage, though for Weber it might be more accurate to call it a paroxysm within the cage. Such an attitude toward freedom and rationalization is not without danger.

Since 1973, Freedom House, a foundation dedicated to research on freedom, has published the comparative study of freedom, in which it ranks almost every country and territory on earth. The questions (which have changed little in the last 30 years) and the rankings can be found on the Freedom House website, www.freedomhouse.org/ratings. Freedom is defined by Freedom House as constitutionalism, which is why I consider it here. For Freedom House, freedom means constitutionally guaranteed rights of political participation and civil liberties, rights that are both entrenched and enforced (Gastil, 1991). Otherwise expressed, Freedom House defines freedom as the presence of constitutionally entrenched democratic institutions, even though Raymond Gastil, who created the survey, says he remains open to the possibility of freedom in the absence of democracy (1991, 22).

In spite of employing a restricted definition of freedom, the Freedom House project is important. If one is going to compare over one hundred countries, one needs fairly simple and straightforward measures of freedom. Furthermore, it is important to make the effort, lest we treat freedom as though it were an ineffable presence that can never be measured. If freedom can never be measured, then how could anyone know they don't have it?

"The main thing is to learn to think crudely (*das plumpe Denken*)," said Bertolt Brecht. "Crude thoughts . . . should be part and parcel of dialectical thinking, because they are nothing but the referral of theory to practice" (Arendt, 1968, 168). Freedom House's comparative survey of freedom is crude thinking, a necessary part of what it means to reflect critically on freedom, lest we make freedom so subtle it can never be measured. Sometimes it is good to measure, especially when what is being measured is not the beliefs of citizens, which are rarely crude, but the practices of regimes. Seen from the perspective of constitutionalism, it might make more sense to argue that Freedom House is measuring not the presence or absence of freedom but the material and social conditions under which men and women are most likely to experience freedom. In fact, this is basically what Gastil says (1991, 22–23).

Imagine my disappointment when I tried to interview someone connected with Freedom House. In e-mails and telephone calls I explained my research, asking if anyone at Freedom House would be willing to be interviewed about my results, which are (roughly) that many young people don't believe they are free because:

(1) They are slaves to a job, to making a living.
(2) They work in, go to school in, and daily deal with giant, unresponsive bureaucracies.
(3) They fear they are stuck in their social class (middle, middle, middle) for the rest of their lives.
(4) They are daily disciplined by experts, though of course they do not use Foucault's language.

I'd be interested, I said, to know what someone at Freedom House thought about the responses of the young people I spoke with: were they immature, self-indulgent, lacking in historical knowledge and global context? Or did these young people understand something about freedom that couldn't be readily measured? Gastil (1991, 22–23, 37) would likely be sympathetic to this last view. Portions of his essay on his survey's methodology suggest he would.

No one at Freedom House wanted to talk with me. One senior staff person said they couldn't see any connection between what I was doing and what they do, so what was the point? The press officer didn't return my calls. Freedom House was unable to see the relevance of a most important question. How to understand young people's experiences of unfreedom so as to make a connection between their experiences and politics, a politics that is at least on the same page as the politics with which Freedom House is concerned, the politics of constitutionalism?

Making the connection is difficult, but it is the proper path of anyone who would make politics relevant to a new generation. The path runs from appreciating (within real limits) young people's views of freedom to a concern with how their views might be authentically politicized. The term "authentically politicized" refers to how one might talk about a politics of freedom that would seem relevant to young people, given their views on freedom. Telling people that they should be sure and vote in every election and always to practice free speech would not be relevant. Talking with people about how disciplinary power is vulnerable to transgression with others might be. In any case, my goal is not to redefine freedom as a subjective experience but to connect this experience with the real world people live in. About this connection (or even that a connection needs to be made), the people at Freedom House had not a clue.

Seeing Freedom Clearly

For Tocqueville, the modern world is at risk of being emptied of meaning not because Enlightenment disenchants the world (though it does) but because equality of condition results in the loss of singularity, difference, and distinction. In a homogenized, one-dimensional world, Fate and Might rule as though they were gods, as there are no other values left to oppose them. Or rather, all other values are rendered one, each equal to all the rest. As the sun puts all the stars to shame (Hobbes's image of the power of the sovereign), so Fate and Might render all other values equally insignificant. Power rules, but only because it is lucky.

Participation in power through transgression with others is not the freedom most people have in mind. Not participation in power but just power, on the basis of which they can finally relax—this is the image of freedom of most I spoke with. It is hard to say they are wrong. Though Cicero and Nader were quoted, it would be incorrect to conclude that freedom is participation in power if that implies that it is the participation itself that is freedom. No, participation in power through transgression with others fosters freedom for it teaches a lesson about individual power-lessness and dependence in mass society in a way that avoids inflicting so much narcissistic injury that the lesson cannot be endured. Or perhaps one should just say that the narcissistic injury is made more endurable by the companionship of others like us. Narcissistic injury loves company. Freedom itself remains an achievement of individuals. Not autonomous individuals but dependent ones, but still individuals.

Almost nothing in the culture helps young people see these things. At this point in the political life of the nation, when all historical alter-natives but one appear exhausted, the political implications of seeing clearly are best understood as fostering a type of informal ideology critique. Not one that says, "don't believe all that you are told about freedom," for people know that already, but a critique that fosters a way of thinking that finds freedom to stretch out and relax in small spaces whose walls are not made entirely of money but from the creative inventiveness of those who live there, able to put the detritus of mass culture together in new ways. These spaces may be as small as that inhabited by Danielle, her husband, and her mother, a petite association practicing freedom.

Seeing freedom as a practice in the world, not just a psychological achievement (though of course it is both at once), is the reason not to conclude that the right attitude can heal the split in freedom, its division into mastery and relaxation. People's thinking about freedom will remain split until the world itself is healed, and even then one wonders. There is something about the experience of freedom itself that lends to thinking about it in terms of losing and fusing. Indeed, one might even define freedom as the ability to move back and forth along this continuum without spending too much time at the extremes, and without getting stuck at any one point along the way. One should, in any case, remain skeptical about the language of healing when applied to politics or freedom. Nothing in the critique of contemporary freedom as a borderline experience should cause us to forget this last point.

RESEARCH APPENDIX

Though a number of older people were interviewed, most are young, and in this regard mine is not a random sample. Interviewed were 35 younger (18–30 years) and 17 older (31–74 years) informants.

As stated in chapter 1, I use the term "informant" because it is a common designation among anthropologists. Particularly with younger informants, I often felt as though I was interviewing members of an unfamiliar tribe with whom I had been living for years without ever noticing their presence.

The median younger informant was 24 years old. Subjects were almost equally divided between men and women. As far as I could tell, the sex of the subject made no difference to how he or she conceived freedom.

Almost all I spoke with were from the middle class, an economic category that covers an enormous range. Several spoke of making decisions that revealed real economic pressure, such as being unable to have a car repaired and so taking the bus. One was a multimillionaire.

With several exceptions, all had at least two years of college. The exceptions were among the most well read of all informants.

Race is a complicated category these days. The men and women interviewed identified themselves with half a dozen racial and religious groups. About 70 percent of the informants were self-identified white. Chapter 1 contains more details on the importance, and unimportance, of ethnicity.

Interviews were not tape recorded. After working through four books and research projects employing in-depth interviews, it has been my experience that the presence of a tape recorder inhibits the speaker, even if he or she says it doesn't. Instead, I take contemporaneous notes.

As part of my research practice, I give my telephone number to everyone I interview, asking them to call if they want to add to or change their answers. Several did.

List of Questions

1. What's freedom?
2. Are you free?
3. Why is freedom good? (wait for answer) Is freedom ever bad?
4. What does it mean to say the United States is a free country? Is it?
5. What's the opposite of freedom?
6. What could make you more free? (wait for answer) Do you think you will

be more free ten years from now?
7. Tell me a story, or give me an image, about freedom.
8. When are you most free? (Elaborate if necessary as "What time of day do you feel most free?")
9. What experience of yours has taught you the most about freedom? It need not be a good experience.
10. What do you want to tell me about freedom?

Each interview lasted for about an hour, sometimes longer. Though each person was asked every question, the interview was conducted in an informal conversational style. Occasionally I challenged a person's answer. Most interviews were conducted in my office on campus, which is fairly comfortable. A number were conducted at informants' homes.

The best interviews were hour-long conversations. The biggest problem was that everyone I spoke with knew that I am a professor of political science, and several seemed overly interested in impressing the professor with their knowledge of the views of John Stuart Mill, and so forth. In the literature on empirical methods this is called a demand performance characteristic. With all but one person, this tendency quickly wore off, so that by the end of the interview it felt like a conversation.

Though I was listening for the narrative structure of freedom in the stories that make up a person's life, this is best brought out in the give and take of conversation. Just asking people to talk about freedom in a general way is not as useful. While it is important to practice silence, it is almost as important to engage the story, occasionally even telling a story of one's own.

Informants were as a group surprisingly revealing about their private lives, referring to everything from abortions to drug use.

All signed a standard consent form approved by my university's Human Subjects Review Committee.

All names are pseudonyms. Except in cases where a person's views were themselves expressive of his or her ethnicity or national background, what might be called "ethnic matching" was not employed, in which the pseudonym is itself a name common to the ethnic group or nationality of the informant. The result is that there are a few more Peter, Paul, and Sallys than was actually the case.

Papers and Panels

In addition to the interviews, 200 young people were asked to write an essay on "What is freedom?" This helped set a context for the interviews and also to get a better sense of whether the people I spoke with were "average." They seemed to be. None of the quotations in this manuscript are from these essays. Essays establish a background but it is the live encounter that counts.

The long quote from the former Korean dissident was contained in an e-mail response to a question I'd asked about freedom. All other quotations are from my notes.

In addition to the interviews and essays, I listened to two groups of young people discuss freedom among themselves for several hours. I've done this in the past and it is a surprisingly good check. Informants are often more critical of each other than I would dare to be, and listening to people defend their views can be useful in discovering the reasoning behind the answer. During interviews, I often challenge people, but not to the degree that their peers do. In addition, there is a dynamic to group discussion that is absent in interviews.

Comparison with the General Social Survey

The General Social Survey (GSS) has been conducted by the National Opinion Research Center at the University of Chicago since 1972. An in-home interview with a national probability sample of 2,817 respondents, the interview covers an enormous range of questions, from house cleaning to living with disabilities. The "freedom module" is new, and exactly half the respondents participated.

As part of my research, 50 younger men and women were asked to answer the same questions as the GSS on freedom. All fit the profile of my informants; one-fifth later became informants. Here are the questions from the GSS, with one or two left out because they were not relevant.

1. How much freedom do Americans have?
2. How much freedom do you have?
3. Do Americans have more freedom than in the past?
4. Are you satisfied with the way democracy works in America?
5. Being left alone is important for freedom.
6. No government interference is important for freedom.
7. A feeling of inner peace is important for freedom.
8. Political participation is important for freedom.
9. A choice of what to do in life is important for freedom.
10. The expression of unpopular ideas is important for freedom.
11. How much choice and control do you feel you have over your own life?
12. The existence of some rich and some poor is ok in a free society.

In general, my respondents answered the GSS in the same way that most people answered the GSS. To be sure, the answers of my respondents are not identical, most probably because they were not drawn from a random sample of the population. My respondents are younger than average, better educated than average, and not as likely to be white as the random sample chosen by the GSS. My respondents were somewhat less likely to say, for example, that Americans have complete freedom. On the other hand, my respondents were more likely to say that the existence of some rich and some poor is compatible with a free society.

My respondents score about 20 percent lower on a couple of questions. For example, on the question, "How much freedom do Americans have?" The GSS has almost 70 percent of respondents answering in the top two categories (complete, a great deal), whereas only 52 percent of respondents in my study answer in the top two categories.

On several other questions, such as "Are you satisfied with the way democracy works in America?" There is almost no difference between the GSS averages and my own.

The two questions that generated the greatest difference were as follows. "Being left alone is important to freedom," and "A feeling of inner peace is important to freedom." On the former question, 78 percent of the GSS respondents answer in the top three categories (most important, extremely important, very important), whereas only 47 percent of respondents in my study do so. On the latter question, 86 percent of GSS respondents answered in the top three categories (most important, extremely important, very important), but only 56 percent of respondents in my study.

Overall, it is not the difference between informants and the GSS random sample that is impressive, but the similarity. Impressive is the difference between answering questions on a survey and talking about one's experience of freedom in a loosely structured interview.

The simplest thing to say is that the two realms of discourse are incommensurable. Informants don't contradict the GSS. Informants talk about freedom in ways that don't fit the categories of the GSS. For example, a number of people said that they are as free as can be but that it hardly matters. What matters is the power to do what one wants. One could argue that this is an elaboration of GSS question two (or perhaps question eleven), what qualitative research can add to its quantitative cousin, a distinction between freedom and power. It would be more accurate to say that the GSS and my qualitative research are tapping ways of thinking about freedom that hardly overlap at all.

Interviewing several informants who also took the GSS, I asked them if they would tell me how they answered a couple of questions on the GSS. They did, and there is no reason to doubt their honesty; this was not a touchy subject. When I pointed out that there seemed to be discrepancies between what they said in the extended interview and how they answered on the GSS, one person responded this way. "One doesn't really have much to do with the other, does it? The questions you gave us, they were about what people think in general. But when you asked me about freedom, then I told you about what I think." It is as though the informant answered the GSS in his role as "average American citizen," whereas he responded to my questions as "Cliff." Perhaps that's the way it works with most surveys—respondents imaginatively identifying with the role of average citizen of this or that type.

In any case, my study neither supplements nor supplants the survey research on freedom. My study draws upon and reflects a different universe of discourse about freedom, one that hardly fits the usual categories.

NOTES

Chapter 1 Freedom or Power?

1. Cultural anthropologists distinguish between emic and etic approaches to understanding an unfamiliar culture. (The terms stem from the attempt to extend linguistic analysis to the social domain. Emic is drawn from phonemic and etic from phonetic. For most anthropologists, the linguistic origins of the terms are no longer controlling.) An emic analysis tries to see the culture as its members see it, generally using the language and concepts of those who are being studied. Emic analysis attempts to understand a society from inside out, much as the societal members understand their own society, using many of the terms and concepts employed by societal members in their everyday lives. Etic analysis, on the other hand, uses the anthropologist's own conceptual categories, which may not correspond to the way the societal members explain events. My approach combines emic and etic. Emic characterizes freedom in terms of both mastery and relaxation, using the categories of informants. Interpreting these characterizations as being marked by a split, similar to that of borderline thinking, as psychologists call it, is etic. Telling people that I see their accounts as marked by this split, in order to see if they themselves are aware of it, is a combination of these two approaches, aimed at determining whether a version of my etic analysis makes sense to them. In other words, is a version of my etic analysis already part of informants' emic analysis, even if we do not use the same terms? For many it is.
2. One way to think about freedom is that it is an "essentially contested concept." With that term, W. B. Gallie (1962) refers to concepts that participate in a tradition of conflicting interpretations so fundamental that they are permanent and without resolution. Gallie himself uses the example of the "best" bowling team. If all agreed that the best team was the one that scored highest in the tournament, the resolution would be easy. But if one team thinks "best" means the fastest bowlers and another team thinks "best" means the most stylish bowlers—those who release the ball with the greatest flourish—then resolution is impossible. To be sure, each side can talk with each other. The conflict is not beyond rational discussion, for each side can give reasons for its standards. The conflict is just not rationally decidable.
3. Following Wittgenstein (1961, 6:53–57), I make no distinction between terms, words, and concepts, as though the concept of freedom were more powerful than the word. The problem of freedom will not be solved with verbal distinctions.

4. It must, of course, have been a more complicated story. Many of the famous women of Greek tragedy are hardly passive and submissive, which is why they are so frightening. Consider Antigone, Clyteaemestra, and Medea. Nor was Pericles' mistress, Aspasia, silent, passive, and submissive, which is why Thucydides is probably making a joke about her (*History*, 2.46).

Chapter 2   Borderlines of Freedom

1. <www.promisekeepers.org/resc/resc130.htm>. Those familiar with the philosophy of Michel Foucault (1979) will recognize the similarity between "Eye Promise" and the Panopticon, Jeremy Bentham's image of the all-seeing prison guard tower, adopted by Foucault as icon of unfreedom in the modern world. Striking is how eager some people are to fall under its all-seeing gaze. More on this point in chapter 6.

2. This interview took place before September 11, 2001. Had it taken place afterward, Gregory might have worried about human hands blowing apart the bridge. But perhaps not. In general, I was surprised how issues associated with terrorism and freedom seldom came up in the interviews conducted after September 11, 2001. See the Research Appendix for more on this point.

3. Even MacIntyre restricts himself to the dependencies characteristic of infancy, illness, and old age, as though dependency were restricted to the sick, the young, and the old.

4. The language of container and contained is the language of the psychoanalyst and group theorist Wilfred Bion (1970).

5. Liddell and Scott's *Intermediate Lexicon* on the web <www.perseus.tufts.edu> provides word counts for many important Greek words. *Eleutheros* is the second most-common Greek word for freedom, suggesting not the domination of self and others but release, such as release from pain or suffering. The Greeks possessed the semantic subtlety to put it differently had they wanted.

Chapter 3   Bad Faith?

1. Lloyd spoke with me several years ago. He was not part of this study.

2. Hannah Arendt (2000, 455) recognizes that the "new Stoicism" must make a mockery of freedom, as it willfully ignores the difficult to bear, but overwhelmingly obvious, fact that I live among others.

> Under human conditions, which are determined by the fact that not man but men live on the earth, freedom and sovereignty are so little identical that they cannot even exist simultaneously. When men wish to be sovereign, as individuals or as organized groups, they must submit to the oppression of the will, be this the individual will with which I force myself, or by the "general will" of an organized group. If men wish to be free, it is precisely sovereignty they must renounce.

3. In fact, the ideal of shared freedom begins on the last pages of *Being and Nothingness* (1956, 797–798), where Sartre wonders if freedom might itself

become a universal value. A few years later, in "The Humanism of Existentialism," Sartre (1999, 58) agrees with Kant "that freedom desires both itself and the freedom of others," even if Sartre's reasoning differs from Kant's.

4. The assumption that responsibility equals freedom does not define existentialism. Though he is often classified as one, Albert Camus held that he was not an existentialist (1960, 58). Writing in "Bread and Freedom," Camus stated that it is not responsibility but struggle that defines freedom in a world in which freedom must "be won every day by the effort of each and the union of all" (1960, 97). Charming and humane as it is, Camus' position is not mine either.

Chapter 4   Mastery and Respite

1. *Madame Bovary* was written by Gustave Flaubert and was published in 1856.
2. The main reason that Plato so loved and admired Socrates is that Socrates was invulnerable to *tuche* (fate or chance). To be sure, Socrates could be killed but he could not be harmed: nothing could make him a bad person and nothing could make him unhappy. This is the point of several dialogues, including *The Republic*, especially 441d–449a.
3. Marcuse (1966, 162) quotes from a portion of this Sonnet, the first Elegy, and it is Marcuse's translation employed here, a translation based on that by Jessie Lemont, translator of *Sonnets to Orpheus: Duino Elegies* (1945).
4. Not starvation but social marginalization so extreme that they were without health insurance or retirement benefits, forced to live in cheap apartments and work at unskilled jobs, was the fate of many whistleblowers I studied for a previous book (Alford, 2001). All were once well-paid professionals.
5. The term Marcuse (1970) uses to describe this psychological effect is the "massification of domination." "Massification" refers to the disappearance of any inner space of resistance, the result of having to fight for one's freedom. What Sartre calls *Néant* is similar to this inner space.
6. For my discussion of income inequality in America, I draw heavily upon Paul Krugman (2002).
7. Gretchen Morgenson (2004) refers to a study in 2000 by Towers Perrin. In the United States, the CEO of big domestic companies makes 531 times the pay of the average employee. Next on the list of greatest disproportion between CEO and worker is Brazil at 57 times, and then Mexico at 45 times. In Britain, the CEO makes 25 times more than the average employee, in France 16 times, and in Japan 11 times. Depending on how you count, the details differ but the lesson remains the same.
8. Data supporting this conclusion are drawn from a national survey conducted jointly by *The Washington Post*, the Henry J. Kaiser Family Foundation, and Harvard University, carried out in 2002, and reported in *The Washington Post* by Goldstein and Morin (2002).
9. Bush's comments on Berg were delivered on May 12, 2004 and can be found on the White House website <www.whitehouse.gov/news/releases/2004/05/20040512-2.html>. There he says, "The actions of the terrorists who executed this man remind us of the nature of the few people who want

to stop the advance of freedom in Iraq." Bush's earlier comments on "these people hate freedom, and we love freedom" are found in *The Washington Post*, April 7, 2004, A1.

10. United States Department of Education archives <www.ed.gov/news/pressre-leases/2001/10/10302001.html>.

Chapter 5   Freedom Is Seeing Reality Clearly

1. Such a view of freedom is often called evaluative freedom. As William Schweiker (1995, 144) puts it, "an evaluative theory [of freedom] argues that an agent is free if and only if she or he acts on what is most basically valued, what really matters to her or him, and not simply what is desired or wanted." Evaluative freedom is an instance of compatibilism, which seeks to make determinism and moral responsibility compatible. Hegel is the most famous exponent of compatibilism. For Hegel, the dualism, or conflict, between individual morality and social institutions is only apparent. Modern institutions such as the family, civil society, and state, do not require duties in conflict with my individual ends. Rather, these institutions are the realization of individual free will. If one had known the course of history and if one had the power to change it, one would have made it the way it is. This is the context of Hegel's famous saying "what is rational is actual and what is actual is rational" (Hegel, 1967, 10). Not all versions of compatibilism are as quick to equate social constraint with freedom.

2. Is seeing reality clearly an act of free will? For Murdoch, the will is shaped by what we see rather than determining what we see. In other words, Murdoch's view comes closer to Socrates' "no one does wrong knowingly" than to Saint Augustine. Nevertheless, Murdoch recognizes that will may influence what we pay attention to and hence what we see. There is, thus, in Murdoch a version of *akrasia* (weakness of the will to do what is right), but it has more the quality of weakness of vision, the distortion of vision by egoism and fantasy. As David Gordon (1995, 61, 68) observes, for Murdoch, unlike Augustine, "original sin" refers not to the perversity of the will but to the distortion of vision by vanity and egoism. This is why "unselfing" is the royal road to virtue. "Unselfing" breaks open the ego, unfolding it so that it may encounter the reality of others. Not the direct perception of the reality of others but the imaginary perception, unbiased by vanity and fancy (Murdoch, 1970, 48). When this happens, we may say not that will has been vanquished but that it has been absorbed into attention. That, for Murdoch, is the true meaning of free will.

3. "Soulagement" is the term used by Nussbaum (2001, 187), following the psychoanalyst Christopher Bollas.

Chapter 6   Transgression with Others

1. George Kateb made these points at a small conference on the Psychology of Civil Society, sponsored by the Civil Society Initiative at the University of Maryland, and convened by James Glass and myself. The participants were

Richard Flathman, George Kateb, Jane Mansbridge, Nancy Rosenblum, Eric Uslaner, Mark Warren, and Clyde Wilcox. Most would probably disagree with my conclusions.

2. In *Tocqueville Between Two Worlds*, Sheldon Wolin (2001, 378) argues that the role of association changes between the two volumes of *Democracy in America* (the second volume was written five years after the first). "From participatory practices as the center of a flourishing politics to associations as defensive in an apolitical setting," is how Wolin characterizes this change. More on this point in the next chapter.

3. Relativism is a poor argument for tolerance because, from the fact that one cannot distinguish among beliefs on the basis of their truthfulness or rightness, one might as readily conclude that all beliefs should be suppressed as conclude that none should be. Or, that a lottery or whim should decide on what one is allowed to profess. Similarly, the fact that talents and resources are arbitrarily distributed does not imply that they should be more meaningfully distributed. Robert Nozick (1977) makes much of this point. My interpretation of Rawls follows closely that of Michael Sandel (1982) in *Liberalism and the Limits of Justice*.

4. I don't know whether this is the full medical story but it doesn't matter in this context. Not medical truth but the social reality of Lumara and her family is my concern. My account is based solely on my interview with Lumara.

5. Personal communication with Rosenblum.

6. Several authors, including John McGowan (1998, 85–88), have noticed the similarity between Arendt and Foucault on this point, both coming shockingly close to assimilating bureaucracy and administration to totalitarianism.

7. The poem is Frost's "The Tuft of Flowers."

Chapter 7   Aristocrats of Freedom

1. Conradi's (2001a, 312) biography of Iris Murdoch claims she had a brief but intense love affair with Oakeshott. While Murdoch shared Oakeshott's opposition to rationalism in politics, she disliked his distrust of utopias, calling his a "lazy philosophy based on refusal to think or do anything." In any case, phenomenal freedom seems predicated on seeing oneself and others clearly.

2. Seeing freedom as *arête* gives new meaning to Aristotle's interpretation of *arête* as a doctrine of the mean, which he also understood to have nothing to do with the middle in a literal or mathematical sense; for Aristotle, the middle is metaphor (*N. Ethics* 1105b20–1109b25).

3. The general symmetry conditions of discourse, as Habermas calls them, require that every participant have: (1) the same chance to initiate and perpetuate a discourse; (2) the same chance to put forward, call into question, justify, or refute statements, so that in the long run no statement is immune to criticism; (3) the same chance to express attitudes, feelings, and intentions, so that all may see if the participants are sincere and truthful; (4) the same chance to permit and forbid, so that the formal equality of chances to initiate discourse can actually be realized. These conditions are paraphrased from McCarthy (1973).

4. A discourse without words hardly makes sense in Habermas's project. Discourse remains what it always was for Habermas, the realm in which language lives a life of its own, carrying its speakers with it, what Habermas (1979) once called the telos of truth implicit in every speech act.

5. The quote is from the entry on "Constitutionalism" in the *Stanford Encyclopedia of Philosophy*, written by Will Waluchow <http://plato.standford.edu>. The example of the election in Florida is from this entry.

6. In *The Experience of Freedom*, Jean-Luc Nancy (1998) writes that freedom is an exposure to groundlessness, "the experience of experience." Freedom is an experience of surprise at an existence that appears from no place and means nothing, not even that man is essentially free. Freedom just is (xxii-xxiii). With Nancy's study of the experience of freedom there is much to agree. Freedom isn't so much an experience of this or that as it is surrender to a certain type of experience. Nancy's conclusion, however, seems mistaken. Politics, he concludes, cannot secure freedom because the experience of freedom is antithetical to any type of grounding or founding, including that of constitutions and institutions. Any attempt to secure freedom must reify it, and so poison the source of its fluidity. Nancy does not take his own conclusion seriously enough. If the experience of freedom is groundlessness, an experience of experience, then the political institutions of freedom are not reifications of freedom but freedom's enabling condition. The first ten amendments to the Constitution of the United States—the Bill of Rights—are not freedom. They create conditions under which people may (but not necessarily will) experience freedom.

REFERENCES

Note: references to classical sources in the text given in the form that is usual in classical studies are not repeated here.

Adorno, Theodor. 1974. *Minima Moralia*, translated by E. F. N. Jephcott. London, UK: New Left Books.

———. 1978. "Subject and Object," in *The Essential Frankfurt School Reader*, edited by Andrew Arato and Eike Gebhardt, pp. 497–511. New York: Urizen Books. (The essay originally appeared in Adorno's *Stichworte*, 1969.)

Alford, C. Fred. 1997. *What Evil Means to Us*. Ithaca, NY: Cornell University Press.

———. 1999. *Think No Evil: Korean Values in the Age of Globalization*. Ithaca, NY: Cornell University Press.

———. 2001. *Whistleblowers: Broken Lives and Organizational Power*. Ithaca, NY: Cornell University Press.

American Psychiatric Association. 2000. *Diagnostic and Statistical Manual of Mental Disorders*, 4th edition. Washington, D.C.: Author.

Antonaccio, Maria. 2000. *Picturing the Human: The Moral Thought of Iris Murdoch*. Oxford: Oxford University Press.

Arendt, Hannah. 1968. *Men in Dark Times*. New York: Harcourt, Brace and World.

———. 1998. *The Human Condition*, 2nd edition. Chicago, IL: University of Chicago Press.

———. 2000. "What is Freedom?" in *The Portable Hannah Arendt*, edited by Peter Baehr, pp. 438–461. New York: Penguin Books.

Bay, Christian. 1970. *The Structure of Freedom*. Stanford, CA: Stanford University Press.

Bellah, Robert et al. 1985. *Habits of the Heart: Individualism and Commitment in American Life*. Berkeley, CA: University of California Press.

Benjamin, Jessica. 1988. *The Bonds of Love: Psychoanalysis, Feminism, and the Problem of Domination*. New York: Pantheon Books.

Berlin, Isaiah. 1969. "Two Concepts of Liberty," in *Four Essays on Liberty*, pp. 118–172. Oxford: Oxford University Press. [Includes author's introduction, ix–lxiii.]

Bion, Wilfred. 1970. *Attention and Interpretation*. New York: Basic Books.

Bloom, Allan. 1979. "Introduction" to *Emile*, translated by Allan Bloom. New York: Basic Books.

———. 1998. *The Closing of the American Mind*. New York: Touchstone Books.

Brooks, David. 2001. "The Organization Kid." *The Atlantic Monthly*, April.

Camus, Albert. 1960. *Resistance, Rebellion and Death*, translated by Justin O'Brien. New York: Vintage.

Cohen, Paul M. 1997. *Freedom's Moment: An Essay on the French Idea of Liberty from Rousseau to Foucault*. Chicago, IL: University of Chicago Press.

Conradi, Peter. 2001a. *Iris Murdoch: A Life*. New York: W.W. Norton,

———. 2001b. *The Saint and the Artist: A Study of the Fiction of Iris Murdoch*. New York: Harper Collins.

Farr, Anthony. 1998. *Sartre's Radicalism and Oakeshott's Conservatism: The Duplicity of Freedom*. New York: St. Martin's Press.

Finley, John Huston. 1967. *Three Essays on Thucydides*. Cambridge: Harvard University Press.

Flathman, Richard. 2003. *Freedom and Its Conditions: Discipline, Autonomy, and Resistance*. New York: Routledge

Flax, Jane. 1991. *Thinking Fragments: Psychoanalysis, Feminism, and Postmodernism in the Contemporary West*. Berkeley, CA: University of California Press.

Foner, Eric. 1998. *The Story of American Freedom*. New York: W.W. Norton.

Foucault, Michel. 1979. *Discipline and Punish: The Birth of the Prison*, translated by Alan Sheridan. New York: Vintage Books.

———. 1984. "What is Enlightenment?" translated by Catherine Porter, in *The Foucault Reader*, edited by Paul Rabinow, pp. 32–50. New York: Pantheon Books.

Fourier, Charles. 1971. *Design for Utopia: Selected Writings of Charles Fourier*. New York: Schocken Books.

Freud, Anna. 1966. *The Ego and the Mechanisms of Defense*, revised edition, translated by Cecil Baines. New York: International Universities Press. [Volume 2 of *The Writings of Anna Freud*.]

Freud, Sigmund. 1959. *Group Psychology and the Analysis of the Ego*, translated by James Strachey. New York: W.W. Norton.

———. 1961. *Civilization and Its Discontents*, translated by James Strachey. New York: W.W. Norton.

Fromm, Erich. 1969. *Escape from Freedom*. New York: Harry Holt.

Gallie, W. B. 1962. "Essentially Contested Concepts," in *The Importance of Language*, edited by Max Black, pp. 121–146. Englewood Cliffs, NJ: Prentice-Hall.

Gastil, Raymond, 1991. "The Comparative Survey of Freedom: Experiences and Suggestions," in *On Measuring Democracy*, edited by Alex Inkeles, pp. 21–46. New Brunswick, NJ: Transaction Publishers.

Goldstein, Amy and Morin, Richard. 2002. "Young Voters' Disengagement Skews Politics." *The Washington Post*, October 20, A1.

Gordon, David. 1995. *Iris Murdoch's Fables of Unselfing*. Columbia, MO: University of Missouri Press.

Greenbaum, T. 1978. "The 'Analyzing Instrument' and the 'Transitional Object,'" in *Between Reality and Fantasy*, edited by S. Grolnick and I. Barkin, pp. 191–202. New York: Jason Aronson.

Greenberg, Jay and Mitchell, Stephen. 1983. *Object Relations in Psychoanalytic Theory*. Cambridge: Harvard University Press.

Habermas, Jürgen. 1970. "The Scientization of Politics and Public Opinion," in *Toward a Rational Society*, translated by Jeremy Shapiro, pp. 62–80. Boston, MA: Beacon Press.

———. 1979. "Historical Materialism and the Development of Normative Structures," in *Communication and the Evolution of Society*, translated by Thomas McCarthy, pp. 96–129. Boston, MA: Beacon Press.

———. 1998. *The Inclusion of the Other: Studies in Political Theory*, edited by Ciaran Cronin and Pablo De Greiff. Cambridge: MIT Press.

Hadot, Pierre. 2002. *What Is Ancient Philosophy?* translated by Michael Chase. Cambridge, MA: The Belknap Press of Harvard University Press.

Hampshire, Stuart. 1975. *Freedom of the Individual*. London, UK: Chatto and Windus.

Hegel, Georg Wilhelm Friedrich. 1967. *Philosophy of Right*, translated by T. M. Knox. London, UK: Oxford University Press.

———. 1971. *Hegel's Philosophy of Mind*, translated by A. V. Miller. Oxford: Clarendon Press. [From *Encyclopedia*, section 482.]

Hobbes, Thomas. 1968. *Leviathan*, edited by C. B. Macpherson. Harmondsworth, UK: Penguin Books.

———. 1991. "Philosophical Rudiments Concerning Government and Society," in *Man and Citizen*, edited by B. Gert. Indianapolis, IN: Hackett. ["Philosophical Rudiments" is often known by its Latin title, *De Cive*.]

Hochschild, Jennifer L. 1981. *What's Fair? American Beliefs about Distributive Justice*. Cambridge: Harvard University Press.

Horkheimer, Max and Adorno, Theodor. 2002. *Dialectic of Enlightenment*, translated by Edmund Jephcott. Stanford, CA: Stanford University Press.

Kant, Immanuel. 1981. *Grounding for the Metaphysics of Morals*, translated by J. Ellington. Indianapolis, IN: Hackett.

Kateb, George. 1992. *The Inner Ocean: Individualism and Democratic Culture*. Ithaca, NY: Cornell University Press.

Kernberg, Otto. 1985. *Borderline Conditions and Pathological Narcissism*. Northvale, NJ: Jason Aronson.

———. 1995. "Hatred as a Core Affect of Aggression," in *The Birth of Hatred: Developmental, Clinical, and Technical Aspects of Intense Aggression*, edited by Salman Akhtar, Selma Kramer, and Henri Parens, pp. 54–82. Northvale, NJ: Jason Aronson.

Krugman, Paul. 2002. "For Richer." *The New York Times Magazine*. October 20.

Lasch, Christopher. 1979. *The Culture of Narcissism*. New York: Warner Books.

Lewin, Roger and Schulz, Clarence. 1992. *Losing and Fusing: Borderline Transitional Object and Self Relations*. Northvale, NJ: Jason Aronson.

Loconte, Joseph. 2004. "Wilson, FDR, Truman, Bush: A 'Messianic Militarist' in the White House? It's Happened Before." *The Wall Street Journal Editorial Page*, electronic edition, original May 14 <www.opinionjournal.com/taste/?id = 110005078>.

MacIntyre, Alasdair. 1981. *After Virtue*. Notre Dame, IN: University of Notre Dame Press.

———. 1999. *Dependent Rational Animals*. Chicago, IL: Open Court.

Marcuse, Herbert. 1964. *One-Dimensional Man*. Boston, MA: Beacon Press.

Marcuse, Herbert. 1965a. "Repressive Tolerance," in *A Critique of Pure Tolerance*, with Robert Paul Wolff and Barrington Moore, Jr. Boston, MA: Beacon Press.

———. 1965b. "Über die philosophischen Grundlagen des wirtschaftswissenschaftslichen Arbeitsbegriffs," in *Kultur und Gesellschaft*, volume 2, pp. 7–48. Frankfurt a.M.: Suhrkamp. [Reprinted in *Herbert Marcuse: Schriften*, volume 1, pp. 407–455. Frankfurt a.M.: Suhrkamp, 1978.]

———. 1966. *Eros and Civilization: A Philosophical Inquiry into Freud*. Boston, MA: Beacon Press.

———. 1969. *An Essay on Liberation*. Boston, MA: Beacon Press.

———. 1970. *Five Lectures: Psychoanalysis, Politics, and Utopia*, translated by Jeremy Shapiro and Shierry Weber. Boston, MA: Beacon Press.

———. 1972. *Counterrevolution and Revolt*. Boston, MA: Beacon Press.

———. 1973. "Sartre's Existentialism," in *Studies in Critical Philosophy*, translated by Joris de Bres, pp. 157–190. Boston, MA: Beacon Press.

———. 1978. *The Aesthetic Dimension: A Critique of Marxist Aesthetics*. Boston, MA: Beacon Press.

Marx, Karl. 2002. *Marx's Eighteenth Brumaire: (Post) Modern Interpretations*, edited by James Martin and Mark Cowling. London, UK: Pluto Press.

McCarthy, Thomas. 1973. "A Theory of Communicative Competence." *Philosophy of the Social Sciences*, vol. 3: 135–156.

McGowan, John. 1998. *Hannah Arendt: An Introduction*. Minneapolis: University of Minnesota Press.

Mill, John Stuart. 1975. *On Liberty*, edited by David Spitz. New York: W.W. Norton.

Miller, James. 1993. *The Passion of Michel Foucault*. New York: Simon and Schuster.

Momigliano, Arnaldo. 1979. "Persian Empire and Greek Freedom," in *The Idea of Freedom: Essays in Honour of Isaiah Berlin*, edited by Alan Ryan, pp. 139–152. Oxford: Oxford University Press.

Morgenson, Gretchen. 2004. "Explaining (or Not) Why the Boss Is Paid so Much." *The New York Times*, January 25, 2004, section 3, 1.

Murdoch, Iris. 1966. *The Time of the Angels*. New York: Viking.

———. 1970. *The Sovereignty of Good*. London, UK: Routledge.

———. 1973. *The Black Prince*. London, UK: Penguin.

———. 1978. *The Sea, the Sea*. London, UK: Penguin.

———. 1987. *Sartre: Romantic Rationalist*. New York: Penguin.

———. 1992. *Metaphysics as a Guide to Morals*. London, UK: Penguin.

———. 1993. *The Green Knight*. New York: Penguin.

———. 1999a. "The Sublime and the Good," in *Existentialists and Mystics: Writings on Philosophy and Literature*, edited by Peter Conradi, pp. 205–220. New York: Penguin Books.

———. 1999b. "The Sublime and the Beautiful Revisited," in *Existentialists and Mystics: Writings on Philosophy and Literature*, edited by Peter Conradi, pp. 261–286. New York: Penguin Books.

Nancy, Jean-Luc. 1993. *The Experience of Freedom*, translated by Bridget McDonald, foreword by Peter Fenves. Stanford, CA: Stanford University Press.

Nietzsche, Friedrich. 1968. *Thus Spoke Zarathustra*, in *The Portable Nietzsche*, edited and translated by Walter Kaufmann, pp. 103–442. New York: Viking.

Nozick, Robert. 1977. *Anarchy, State and Utopia*. New York: Basic Books.

Nussbaum, Martha. 1986. *The Fragility of Goodness: Luck and Ethics in Greek Tragedy and Philosophy.* Cambridge: Cambridge University Press.

———. 1990. *Love's Knowledge: Essays on Philosophy and Literature.* Oxford: Oxford University Press.

———. 2001. *Upheavals of Thought: The Intelligence of Emotions.* Cambridge: Cambridge University Press.

Oakeshott, Michael. 1991. *Rationalism in Politics and Other Essays.* Indianapolis: Liberty Fund.

Orwell, George. 1949. *Nineteen Eighty-Four.* New York: Signet.

Patton, Cindy. 1990. *Inventing AIDS.* London, UK: Routledge.

Pitkin, Hanna Fenichel. 1998. *The Attack of the Blob: Hannah Arendt's Concept of the Social.* Chicago, IL: University of Chicago Press.

Putnam, Robert. 2000. *Bowling Alone: The Collapse and Revival of American Community.* New York: Simon and Schuster.

Rawls, John. 1971. *A Theory of Justice.* Cambridge: Harvard University Press.

Reinhardt, Mark. 1997. *The Art of Being Free: Taking Liberties with Tocqueville, Marx, and Arendt.* Ithaca, NY: Cornell University Press.

Rilke, Rainer Maria. 1945. *Sonnets to Orpheus: Duino Elegies*, translated by Jessie Lemont. New York: Fine Editions Press.

Rorty, Richard. 1989. *Contingency, Irony, and Solidarity.* Cambridge: Cambridge University Press.

———. 1993. "Paroxysms and Politics." *Salgamundi*, vol. 97: 63–64.

Rosenblum, Nancy. 1998. *Membership and Morals: The Personal Uses of Pluralism in America.* Princeton, NJ: Princeton University Press.

Rousseau, Jean-Jacques. 1979. *Emile: or On Education*, translated by Allan Bloom. New York: Basic Books.

Sandel, Michael. 1982. *Liberalism and the Limits of Justice.* Cambridge: Cambridge University Press.

———. 1996. *Democracy's Discontent: America in Search of a Public Philosophy.* Cambridge, MA: The Belknap Press of Harvard University Press.

Sartre, John-Paul. 1956. *Being and Nothingness*, translated by Hazel Barnes. New York: Washington Square Press.

———. 1963. *Saint Genet: Actor and Martyr*, translated by Bernard Frechtman. New York: Mentor Books.

———. 1964 [1938]. *Nausea*, translated by Lloyd Alexander. New York: New Directions.

———. 1974. "The Itinerary of a Thought," in *Between Existentialism and Marxism*, translated by J. Mathews. London, UK: New Left Books.

———. 1981. *The Family Idiot*, vol. 1, translated by Carol Cosman. Chicago, IL: University of Chicago Press.

———. 1999. "The Humanism of Existentialism," in *John-Paul Sartre: Essays in Existentialism*, edited by Wade Baskin, pp. 31–62. Secaucus, NJ: Carol Publishing Group.

———. 2003. *Critique of Dialectical Reason*, vol. 1, translated by A Sheridan-Smith. London, UK: Verso Books.

Schumacher, E. F. 1999. *Small Is Beautiful: Economics as if People Mattered: 25 Years Later, with Commentaries.* Point Roberts, WA: Hartley and Marks.

Schweiker, William. 1995. *Responsibility and Christian Ethics*. Cambridge: Cambridge University Press.

Shapiro, Walter. 2003. "Hype and Glory: Case for Freedom is Compelling if Bush Chooses to Make It." *USA Today*, November 6.

Shklar, Judith. 1989. "The Liberalism of Fear," in *Liberalism and the Moral Life*, edited by Nancy Rosenblum, pp. 21–38. Cambridge: Harvard University Press.

Skocpol, Theda. 1999. "Advocates without Members: Recent Transformation of American Civic Life," in *Civic Engagement in American Democracy*, edited by Theda Skocpol and Morris Fiorina, pp. 461–510. Washington, D.C. and New York: Brookings Institution Press and Russell Sage Foundation.

Smith, Joseph. 1978. "The Psychoanalytic Study of Human Freedom." *Journal of the American Psychoanalytic Association*, vol. 26: 87–107.

Starobinski, Jean. 1988. *Jean-Jacques Rousseau: Transparency and Obstruction*, translated by Arthur Goldhammer. Chicago, IL: University of Chicago Press.

Stephen, James Fitzjames. 1975. "Mill's Fallacies," in *On Liberty: Annotated Text, Sources and Background Criticism*, edited by David Spitz, pp. 142–153. New York: W.W. Norton.

Taylor, Charles. 1975. *Hegel*. New York: Cambridge University Press.

———. 1979. "What's Wrong with Negative Liberty?" in *The Idea of Freedom*, edited by Alan Ryan, 175–193. Oxford: Oxford University Press.

Tocqueville, Alexis de. 2000. *Democracy in America*, edited and translated by Harvey Mansfield and Delba Winthrop. Chicago, IL: University of Chicago Press.

Tyler, Tom. 1998. "Trust and Democratic Governance," in *Trust and Governance*, edited by Valerie Braithwaite and Margaret Levi. New York: Russell Sage Foundation.

Waluchow, Will. 2001. "Constitutionalism," in *The Stanford Encyclopedia of Philosophy* <http://plato.stanford.edu/entries/constitutionalism>.

Weber, Max. 1958. *The Protestant Ethic and the Spirit of Capitalism*, translated by Talcott Parsons. New York: Charles Scribner's Sons.

Weed, F. J. 1993. "The MADD Queen: Charisma and the Founder of Mothers Against Drunk Driving." *Leadership Quarterly*, vol. 43 (3/4): 329–346.

Weil, Simone. 1977a. "The *Iliad*, Poem of Might," in *The Simone Weil Reader*, edited by George Panichas, pp. 153–183. Wakefield, RI: Moyer Bell.

———. 1977b. "The Great Beast," in *The Simone Weil Reader*, edited by George Panichas, pp. 391–396. Wakefield, RI: Moyer Bell.

———. 1977c. "The Love of God and Affliction," in *The Simone Weil Reader*, edited by George Panichas, pp. 439–468. Wakefield, RI: Moyer Bell.

———. 2001. *The Need for Roots: Prelude to a Declaration of Duties Towards Mankind*, translated by Arthur Wills, 2nd edition. New York: Routledge.

Winnicott, Donald W. 1971a. "Transitional Objects and Transitional Phenomena," in *Playing and Reality*, pp. 1–25. London, UK: Routledge.

———. 1971b. "Introduction," in *Playing and Reality*, pp. xi–xiii. London, UK: Routledge.

———. 1986. *Home is Where We Start from: Essays by a Psychoanalyst*, edited by Claire Winnicott, Ray Shepherd, and Madeleine Davis. New York: W.W. Norton.

Wittgenstein, Ludwig. 1961. *Tractatus Logico-Philosophicus*, translated by D. F. Pears and B. F. McGuinnes. New York: Humanities Press.

Wolfe, Alan. (2001). *Moral Freedom: The Search for Virtue in a World of Choice.* New York: W.W. Norton.

Wolin, Sheldon. 1996. "Fugitive Democracy," in *Democracy and Difference: Contesting the Boundaries of the Political,* edited by Seyla Benhabib. Princeton, NJ: Princeton University Press.

———. 2001. *Tocqueville between Two Worlds: The Making of a Political and Theoretical Life.* Princeton, NJ: Princeton University Press.

Wuthnow, Robert. 1999. "Mobilizing Civic Engagement: The Changing Impact of Religious Involvement," in *Civic Engagement in American Democracy,* edited by Theda Skocpol and Morris Fiorina, pp. 331–363. Washington, D.C. and New York: Brookings Institution Press and Russell Sage Foundation.

INDEX

abandonment, 20, 79
action, 23, 96
ACT UP, 112–14, 116, 134, 135
Adorno, Theodor, 64, 68, 74–8, 89,
  92–3, 100, 101, 106, 129
aestheticization of politics, 127
aggression, 78
agon, 19
Alcibiades, 19, 52, 77, 78, 82
alienation, 44
alienation of labor, 70
"all or nothing" thinking, 16–18,
  29, 62
amor fati, 64, 75, 76, 78
anarchists, 7, 15
anomie, 7, 44, 108, 121
Antonaccio, Maria, 90, 97
Arendt, Hannah, 9, 49, 51, 114, 121,
  146n2 (chap. 3), 149n6
arête, 19, 127, 149n2 (chap. 7)
aristocratic freedom, 124–7, 131, 136
Aristotle, 149n2 (chap. 7)
Armey, Richard, 3
art, 33, 35, 92
artist, 93, 95
"art of being free," 111–18, 121
Art of Being Free, The (Reinhardt),
  113–14
association(s), 99–100, 108–9,
  111–14, 117–18, 120–1, 126,
  149n2 (chap. 6)
Atlas Shrugged (Rand), 44
Attack of the Blob, The (Pitkin), 114
attention, 91–2

attunement, 79, 97–8
Augustine, Saint, 148n2
authority, 15, 81, 82
autokratôr, 50–1, 67, 72, 85, 105
autonomy, 3, 38–9, 49–50

Bacon, Francis, 70
"bad faith," 8, 55–6
Bakke decision, 65
balance, 3, 43–8
Baudelaire, Charles, 135
"being alone with another," 37
Being and Nothingness (Sartre), 56,
  60, 65, 97, 146n3 (chap. 3)
Bellah, Robert, 23
Benjamin, Jessica, 39
Bentham, Jeremy, 114,
  146n1 (chap. 2)
Berg, Nicholas, 86, 147n9
Berlin, Isaiah, 15–17, 34, 39, 43, 44
Berlin Wall, fall of, 46, 118
Bill of Rights, 2, 30, 132, 135, 150n6
Bion, Wilfred, 146n4 (chap. 2)
Black Prince, The (Murdoch), 100
Bloom, Alan, 34
Bonfire of the Vanities (Wolfe), 84
Book and the Brotherhood, The
  (Murdoch), 101
borderline experience of freedom,
  see also culture of the borderline;
  losing and fusing
  as "all or nothing," 16–18, 29
  aristocracy of freedom and, 127
  Bush and, 88

borderline experience of freedom—
    continued
    costs of absolute freedom and, 39
    as cultural diagnosis, 8, 27, 28
    cynicism and, 129
    illusion lost in, 32, 61
    losing and fusing poles in, 41–5
    Marcuse and, 67
    rage and, 59–60, 129
    society and, 25
    "transgression with others" and,
        103–4, 106, 111
    transitional space and, 33–4
    will-to-power and, 45
borderline personality disorder, 8, 16,
    27–30, 41
boundaries, absence of, 39–40, 42,
    57, *see also* constraints;
    limitlessness
Bourdieu, Pierre, 100
Bowling Alone (Putnam), 107
"Bread and Freedom" (Camus),
    147n4 (chap. 3)
Brecht, Bertolt, 138
bridge symbol, 37, 46–7
Brooks, David, 13
Buddhism, 92, 93
bureaucracy, 15, 74, 81, 105, 114
Bush, George William, 1,
    86–8, 147n9

Camus, Albert, 147n4 (chap. 3)
capillary power, 126
care, autonomy and, 3
Carel's dark cupboard, 51, 52, 77,
    83–4, 98, 109, 129, *see also*
    fear that force and fate rule
    the world
categorical imperative, 75
causal determinism, 97
CEOs, incomes of, 84, 85, 147n7
"Cheers" (TV show), 107
Cicero, 118, 139

Civilization and Its Discontents
    (Freud), 78
civil liberties, 7
civil society, 75, 118, 132
    association and, 121
    Hobbes on, 50
    self-help groups and, 117–18
    transgression with others versus,
        105, 107–11, 116–17
civil versus natural freedom, 73
Closing of the American Mind, The
    (Bloom), 34
Cohen, Paul, 73–4
collective freedom, 66
"Colours" (song), 37, 80
Comaneci, Nadia, 13
comfort, 21–2, 34
compassion, 92
compatibilism, 75, 148n1 (chap. 5)
concepts, lack of, 23–6
Conradi, Peter, 101, 149n1
consciousnesses, two, 24
conservative critics of freedom, 82
constitution
    as "container," 40
    devaluation of, 132
constitutionalism, 85, 105, 131–9
constraints, 12, 36, 39–40, 63–4,
    74, 75
    internalized, 34, 35, 39–40
consumerism, 12, 112
"container," 40, 146n4 (chap. 2)
Contingency, Irony, and Solidarity
    (Rorty), 136
control, freedom as, 13, 17, 21
convention, 103
    ability to overcome, 91, 94, 95
    aristocratic freedom and, 125
    consumerism and, 112
    mass culture and, 99–100
    phenomenal freedom and, 127–8
    republican political practice and, 99
    young feel trapped in, 63, 98

corporate capitalism, 128
counterculture, 68
countertransference, 31
critical legal theory, 133
critique, 106
Critique of Dialectical Reason
(Sartre), 61
cults, 7
cultural Marxism, 67
culture, 25, 29–30, 32, 33
Culture of Narcissism, The (Lasch), 27,
30, 63
culture of the borderline, 8, 30, 41,
59–60, *see also* borderline
experience of freedom
"cutting out," freedom as, 14, 45
cynicism, 60, 129

death, 19, 77, 78
democracy, 3, 45, 107
Democracy in America (Tocqueville),
3, 45, 107, 124, 126, 136,
149n2 (chap. 6)
"democratic will formation," 130
demographic variables, 5–6
dependence on others, 3, 24, 36–9,
103–4, 116, 119, 146n3
(chap. 2)
absence of, 3, 72–5
transgression with others and, 137
weakness and, 44
Dependent Rational Animals
(MacIntyre), 38
*Diagnostic and Statistical Manual of
Mental Disorders* (*DSM*), 28, 29
disappointment, 30
disciplinary power (discipline), 82,
111, 114–15, 125, 126, 128,
131, 132, 136, 139
discontent of civilization, 36
discourse, 123, 149n3 (chap. 7),
150n4
disillusionment, 35

Donovan, 37, 80
dualism, 75

eastern Europe, 83
economic world
competitiveness of, 25, 121
security and, 81
"the political" and, 123
education, 100, 112
egoism, 45, 110
Electoral College, 133
emic versus etic approaches, 145n1
Emile (Rousseau), 14–15, 73
emotions, 96–8
"empire of might," 52, 57,
85–6, 106
enchantment, 101
English Bill of Rights (1689), 133
enlightenment, 105, 106
"enough," 47
Epictetus, 61, 76
Epicurean freedom, 22–3, 48, 77
wanna-be, 23, 77
equality, 24, *see also* inequality
equality of condition, 109–10, 112,
124–6, 139
Eros, 70–1, 77, 80, 100–1
Eros and Civilization (Marcuse), 78
ethnicity, 6
evaluative freedom, 148n1
(chap. 5)
experience of freedom, 5
concept of freedom versus, 9–15
losing and fusing and, 41–2
splitting and, 25, 27
Experience of Freedom, The (Nancy),
150n6
experiences, lack of concepts to
explain, 23–6
experimental method, 106
"experiments in living," 98–9
experts, 82, 105, 111, 114, 115,
117, 126

extremes, 28–9, *see also* losing and fusing
"Eye Promise," 36, 115, 146n1 (chap. 2)

false-consciousness, 23, 27, 32, 33, 35, 109, 135
Farr, Anthony, 64
fear, 27, 81, 97
  constitutionalism and, 134
fear that force and fate rule the world, 42, 51–2, 57, 59–60, 76, 83–4, 97, 98, 100, 109–10, 139, *see also* Carel's dark cupboard
feminists, 39
Fichte, 119
Flathman, Richard, 128
Flaubert, Gustav, 62, 147n1
Flax, Jane, 39
Foner, Eric, 3, 6
"forced to be free," 36
Ford Expedition, 40
formal or political freedom, 1–2, 6–7, 12, 13, 29, 30
  contempt for, 24
  "freedom with" and, 40
"forward strategy of freedom," 87–8
Foucault, Michel, 74, 82, 106, 111, 114–18, 126, 128, 131, 146n1 (chap. 2), 149n6
Fourier, Charles, 71
Frankfurt School of Critical Theory, 64, 68, 74, 89, 100
free association, 118–21
freedom, *see also* borderline experience of freedom; experience of freedom; formal or political freedom; "freedom with"; mastery freedom as; money; money and power; negative freedom; positive

freedom; power; relaxation or respite, freedom as; splitting of freedom, between mastery and respite; *and other specific concepts and types*
  as actual or nonexistent, 62, *see also* "all or nothing" thinking
  age and definition of, 3–6, 48
  anonymous threats to, 74
  as birthright, 11
  desire for easy and plentiful, 82
  devaluation of, 1, 4, 24, 44
  diversity of people seeing, in same way, 6
  as "essentially contested concept," 145n2
  exemplified by wealthy, 85
  failure to recognize, 8
  informal definitions of, 1
  loss of meaning of, 2–3, 39
  as negative or zero-sum game, 65
  partial, not appreciated, 43
  peak experiences of, as transgression, 119
  regressive urges and, 50
  remembered moments of, 17
  resentment about lack of, 64
  rules and limits that frame, 40
  as skill developed over time, 127
Freedom and Its Conditions (Flathman), 128
Freedom Corps, 86
freedom from fantasy, 92
Freedom House, 137–9
"freedom is not free" cliché, 87
freedom of assembly, 11, 44
freedom of consciousness, 61
freedom of everyday life, 33
freedom of imagination, 33
freedom of press, 11, 44
freedom of religion, 90

freedom of speech, 11, 16, 44, 80, 134
"freedom of the coffee house," 83
Freedom's Moment (Cohen), 73–4
"freedom with," 46–7, 101
  aristocratic freedom and, 124
  defined, 34–7
  dependence and, 103
  Eros versus, 80
  Eye Promise and, 115
  Hegel and, 75
  idealism and, 51
  not imagined by young, 60
  pathological and *outré* forms of, 128–9
  political freedom versus, 40
  Sartre and, 80
  total freedom versus, 39
  transgression with others and, 112
free will, 10, 97, 148n2 (chap. 5)
French Revolution, 82
Freud, Anna, 76
Freud, Sigmund, 28, 36, 37, 58, 67, 70, 78, 119
Fromm, Erich, 128
Frost, Robert, 121, 149n7

Gallie, W. B., 145n2
Gastil, Raymond, 137–9
"gaze, the," 114–15
Geist, 75
General Social Survey (GSS), 4, 5, 85, 143–4
General Will, 35–6, 73, 74
Genet, Jean, 60
global capitalism, 118
Gordon, David, 148n2
Gramsci, Antonio, 24
Great Tradition, 9
Greeks, ancient, 19, 52, 110, 146n5
Green Knight, The (Murdoch), 101
groundlessness, 150n6

Habermas, Jürgen, 129–32, 149n3 (chap. 7), 150n4
Habits of the Heart (Bellah), 23
Haley, Alex, 42
hamartia, 110
"harm principle," 11
health insurance, 84
Hegel, 7, 71, 74–5, 130, 148n1 (chap. 5)
Hispanics, 5
historical alternatives, 119
history, 11, 41
Hitler, 7, 68
HMOs, 111
Hobbes, Thomas, 4, 7, 18, 19, 25, 27, 50, 65, 73, 85, 133
Hockschild, Jennifer, 24
Holy Grail, 91–2
homeowner's association, 112
Horkheimer, Max, 68, 74–8
hot baths, 52, 78
"Humanism of Existentialism, The" (Sartre), 66, 146–7n3 (chap. 3)

idealism, 33, 51, 52
"identification with the aggressor," 76–7
ideology
  critique on, 100, 140
  science and technology as, 131
"ignominious adaptation," 64–5, 76
Iliad, 52
illusion, *see also Néant*
  aristocratic freedom and, 124
  borderline experience and, 41
  inability to use, 33, 34, 51–3, 61
  Marcuse and, 71
  Murdoch and, 93
  transitional experience and, 32–3, 53
  will-to-power and, 44–5
imagination, 17, 29, 33–4, 49, 55, 124
  repressive tolerance and, 82

indebtedness, 135
individual
    associations and, 121
    freedom as achievement of, 127,
        130, 140
individualism, 5–7, 24, 45, 100,
    110–11
    naïve, 12
inequality, 57, 77, 84–5, 147n6
inner freedom, 13–14, 21, 43, 49, 51
inner life
    association and, 120–1
    external reality and, 25
    Stoicism and, 61
insight, 100
institutionalized cruelty, 134
instrumental reason, 131
insults, 11
Intermediate Lexicon (Liddell and
    Scott), 146n5
Internet websites, 6–7
interviews, 27, 30–2, 141–2
    demographics and, 4–5
"in the groove," 34, 35, 53, 80
Iraq war, 86
"Iris" (movie), 89
ironic detachment, 62, 63
Islam, 120, 134
isolation, 7, 21, 44

Jefferson, Thomas, 90
jury nullification, 117

Kant, Immanuel, 20, 60, 66, 73–6,
    92, 121, 146–7n3 (chap. 3)
Kateb, George, 121, 148n1
    (chap. 6)
Kernberg, Otto, 29, 30, 59
knowledge
    emotional response and, 96
    expert power and, 115,
        117, 126
Krugman, Paul, 84–5, 147n6

labor, 69, 70
Lasch, Christopher, 8, 27, 29–31, 63
"Law of the Thing," 69
League for Industrial Democracy, 118
Legitimation Crisis (Habermas), 131
Letter Concerning Toleration, A
    (Locke), 90
Leviathan (Hobbes), 4, 18
Lewin, Roger, 32
liberal concept of freedom, 15–16,
    92, 123, 132
liberal education, 34
Liberalism and the Limits of Justice
    (Sandel), 149n3 (chap. 6)
"Liberalism of Fear" (Shklar), 134
liberal welfare state, 100
Liddell, 146n5
"Lifestyles of the Rich and Famous"
    (TV show), 84
Lightner, Candy, 111
limited sovereignty, 133
limitlessness, 42, 63, *see also*
    boundaries, absence of;
    constraints
limits, intention and, 72
literalism, 18
Locke, John, 90
losing and fusing, 32–43, 140
    avoided by Hegel, 75
    freedom between, 45–6, 48
    illusion and, 32, 61
Losing and Fusing (Lewin and
    Schulz), 32
love, 69, 89, 91–3, 96

McCarthy, 149n3 (chap. 7)
McGowan, John, 149n6
MacIntyre, Alasdair, 38–9, 146n3
    (chap. 2)
Madame Bovary (Flaubert), 67–9,
    100, 147n1
magic, 33, 34, 86–8, 101
Magna Carta, 132

Malcolm X, 8
manic depression, 42
Mao, 67
Marbury v. Madison, 133
Marcuse, Herbert, 8, 23, 33, 42,
  61, 67–72, 77–83, 89, 98,
  100–1, 129, 135, 147n3
  (chap. 4), 147n5
Marx, Karl, 41, 67, 70
mass culture, 34, 98–101, 128, 140
"massification of domination," 147n5
"Masters of the Universe," 84
mastery, freedom as, 7, 9
  abandonment of, in Nietzsche, 75
  aristocratic freedom and, 125
  lives out of control and, 51
  Marcuse's performance principle
    and, 77
  need not be total, 103
  not idealized, but regretted, 30
  as political resource, 83
  real but limited, 127
  splitting of, with relaxation, 20–2,
    24, 27–8, 78, 82
  Stoicism versus, 48–52
  transgression with others and,
    110, 116
materialism, 12
maturation, 46
mature autonomy (*Mündigkeit*), 121
meaning
  giving, as individual, 61–2
  loss of, 57, 97
"meant to do that," 72–80, 128, 130
medicine, 114
Membership and Morals
  (Rosenblum), 113
"message to the individual," 101
Message to the Planet, The
  (Murdoch), 101
Middle East, 87–8
Mill, John Stuart, 10–12, 98, 104,
  107, 121, 126

moeurs, 133
money, 1, 2, 6, 7, 9, 14
  "enough", 47
  freedom unimportant versus, 12
money and power, 13, *see also*
    mastery, freedom as; power
  borderline experience and, 29
  equated, 45
  fear of lacking, 80–1, 85
  freedom as, 6, 49–50, 65–6
  freedom as unimportant versus, 16
moral fear, 3–4
moral freedom, 3
Moral Freedom (Wolfe), 3
moral imagination, 95
moral psychology, 27, 50–1
Morgenson, Gretchen, 147n7
Mothers against Drunk Driving
  (MADD), 111–12
Murdoch, Iris, 8–9, 43, 51–2, 77,
  89–101, 104, 148n2, 149n1
  (chap. 7)

Nader, Ralph, 118, 139
Nancy, Jean-Luc, 150n6
narcissism, 30, 40, 58, 103
  aristocratic freedom and, 125
  association and, 117
  consumerism and, 112
  convention and, 63, 69
  culture of, 8, 29, 30
  liberation from, 94, 95
  mass culture and, 99–100
  Murdoch and, 91–3
  phenomenal freedom and, 127–8
  republican practice and, 99
  will-to-power versus, 44
narcissistic injury, 15, 112, 140
  Western philosophy and avoiding,
    72–80
Narcissus, 71, 72, 75, 77, 79, 82
natural versus civil freedom, 73
nature, 69–71, 73, 79

nausea, 56–7, 59
Nausea (Sartre), 57, 79–80
Nazi party, 97
Néant, 56, 61–3, 69, 75, 80, 89, 96, 100, 147n5
necessity, 52, 70
Need for Roots, The (Weil), 42
negative freedom, 10–11, 17
  Berlin's, 15–16, 43
  phenomenal freedom versus, 128
negotiation of talents, 34–5
neurosis, 91
Nietzsche, 44–5, 64, 75, 76, 78
Nineteen Eighty-Four (Orwell), 33, 100
Nirvana principle, 70
No Exit (Sartre), 69
non-borderline views of freedom, 45–8
Nozick, Robert, 149n3 (chap. 6)
Nussbaum, Martha, 39, 96–7, 148n3

Oakeshott, Michael, 127, 149n1 (chap. 7)
objective reality, 74
object relations theorists, 30
obsessive attachment, 93–5, 99, 103
Odysseus, 71, 79, 82
older people, 3, 46–8, 85
one-dimensionality, 98–9, 125
One-Dimensional Man (Marcuse), 8
On Liberty (Mill), 10, 104
order, 135, 137
"Organization Kid, The" (Brooks), 13
Orpheus, 71, 75, 77, 79, 80, 82
Orwell, George, 33, 100
others, *see also* dependence on others; participation with others; transgression with others
  Murdoch and, 95
  need for, 3, 21, 50, 93
  Rousseau and, 73
  Sartre and, 56, 60, 69

Panopticon, 114–15, 146n1 (chap. 2)
paranoid freedom, 6–7
participation in power, 118–19, 121, 139–40
participation with others, 103–5, 107–9, 125–6, 128
passivity, 19–20, 23, 75, 78, 79
Patton, Cindy, 114
performance principle, 77, 79
permission, not having to ask, 14
permissiveness, 85
Pharisees, 52
phenomenal freedom, 127–8, 149n1 (chap. 7)
Pitkin, Hannah, 114, 121
Plato, 50–1, 72, 76, 104, 128, 147n2
  Murdoch and, 89, 93, 94
play, 69, 70
pleasure, 38
Plutarch, 19
"political, the," 105, 114, 123–7, 132
political freedom, *see* formal or political freedom
politicians, 3
politics, 15, *see also* participation with others
  civil society versus, 121
  freedom as respite and, 83
  Murdoch and, 99–101
  passivity and anger and, 10
  small-scale, 105, 106, 135
  transgression with others and, 40, 104–6, 111, 113–14, 125, 126
  young people and, 139
Port Huron statement (SDS), 118
positive freedom, 17, 34
  Berlin and, 16, 35, 43, 44
  civil society and, 107, 108
  Hobbes and, 50
  phenomenal freedom and, 128
  self-governance and, 99
  will-to-power and, 45
  Wolin and, 136

poststructuralists, 100
potential (being-for-itself), 58, 62
pouvoir social, 125–26
power, 9, *see also* "empire of might";
    fear that fate and force rule the
    world; money and power;
    participation in power
as "all or nothing," 18–19
arbitrariness of, 57
association and, 108
autokratôra and, 50–1
disciplinary versus political, 111
as end goal, in Tocqueville, 6
"enough," 47
of experts and bureaucrats, 105
Foucault and, 114–18
freedom equated with, 1, 4, 7,
    11–12, 14, 31, 46, 59–60,
    63, 66, 97
fusion with, 60, 76, 97
inequality and, 85
money equated with, 45
Nietzsche and, 44–5
as only value, 29, 51–2
performance principle and, 77
politics and social trust and, 121
private, versus governmental,
    136–7
Putnam and, 117–18
revealed, 46
powerlessness, 112, 140
"primacy of the object," 100
privatization, 85
Prometheus, 71
Promise Keepers, 36
Putnam, Robert, 107, 108, 110, 111,
    117–18, 125

radical, limitless freedom as, 63–6
radical politics, 67
rage, 13, 30, 59, 60, 129
Rand, Ayn, 44
rationalism, 129–30

rationalization, 33, 101, 137
Rawls, John, 110, 149n3 (chap. 6)
Reagan, Ronald, 87
reality, *see also* "seeing clearly"
    able to crush any illusion, 51
    being attuned to, 97
    imaginary negation of, 89
    imagination and, 34, 124
    loss of rootedness in, 42
    of other person, put first, 92–9
reason, 129–30
reification of freedom, 134–5, 150n6
Reinhardt, Mark, 113, 117, 121
relativism, 149n3 (chap. 6)
relaxation or respite, freedom as,
    18–28, 52, 77–8, 82, 83, 97,
    116, *see also* sleep, as freedom
    with friends, 20, 78
release, 19, 20, 119
religion, 5, 6, 87, 90
repression, 28
repressive tolerance, 80–3,
    149n3 (chap. 6)
Republic (Plato), 72, 147n2
"republican conception of freedom,"
    99, 104
republican socialism, 123, 133–4
responsibility, 64, 65, 147n4
    (chap. 4)
Rheem, Diane, 2–3
Rilke, Rainer Maria, 79
Rorty, Richard, 136
Rosenblum, Nancy, 113, 117
Rousseau, Jean-Jacques, 14, 35–6,
    72–4, 81

sacred, 33
Sandel, Michael, 90, 94, 99, 104,
    149n3 (chap. 6)
Sartre, Jean-Paul, 8, 23, 55–66,
    69, 71, 74, 75, 79, 89–90,
    95–7, 112, 134, 146–7n3,
    147n5 (chap. 4)

schizoid process, 28, 30
Schulz, Clarence, 32
Schumacher, E. F., 71
Schweiker, William, 148n1 (chap. 5)
science and technology, 114, 131
Scott, 146n5
Sea, the Sea, The (Murdoch), 93
Second Discourse, The (Rousseau),
   72–3
"Securing Freedom's Triumph"
   (Bush), 86
seeing clearly, 93–100, 103, 109,
   111, 124, 125, 128, 131, 148n2
   political implications of, 140
self
   "decreation" of, 42
   encumbered, 90, 94, 96
   higher versus lower, 50–1
   Murdoch and, 93–4, 96–7
   philosophy as defense of, 76–7
   Plato and, 72
self-authorship, 130
self-censorship, 74, 76
self-cultivaton (*Bildung*), 121
self-deception, 93
self-defense, 129
self-discipline, 128
self-help groups, 116–18
self-interest well understood,
   109–12
self-mastery, 51
self-punishment, 36
self-realization, 43
September 11, 2001 attacks, 6,
   146n2 (chap. 2)
shared freedom, 146n3 (chap. 3)
Shklar, Judith, 134
Sirens, 79
Skocpol, Theda, 108
sleep, as freedom, 19–21, 23, 58,
   77–9, 82, *see also* relaxation or
   respite, freedom as
Smith, Joseph, 38

sociability, 82–3, 123
"social, the," 114, 121, 126
social capital, 107, 108, 112, 118
Social Contract, The (Rousseau), 73
social institutions, 75
socialism, 82, 123
social pressure, 11
Social Security, 85
social trust, 107–10, 112, 113, 121
Socrates, 76, 89, 147n2, 148n2
Song Mien, 119, 134
Sonnets to Orpheus (Rilke), 79,
   147n3 (chap. 4)
Sophocles, 38
soulagement, 97, 148n3
South Korean dissidents, 118–19
Soviet Union, 87
splitting of freedom, between mastery
   and respite, 19, 23–9, 41, 43,
   67, 106, 140, *see also* borderline
   experience of freedom; mastery,
   freedom as; relaxation or respite,
   freedom as
Stalin, 7
Starobinski, Jean, 73
state, 74, 75, 85, 112
Stephen, James Fitzjames, 82
Stoicism, 23, 48–53, 61, 76, 128,
   146n2 (chap. 3)
Story of American Freedom, The
   (Foner), 6
Students for a Democratic Society
   (SDS), 118
superego, 36, 115, 128
symbolic freedom, 29, 44, 132
symbols, inability to use, 44, 47–8
"system, the," 81

Taylor, Charles, 27, 75
techné, 94, 104
Theory of Justice, A (Rawls), 110
Time of the Angels, The
   (Murdoch), 51

Tocqueville, Alexis de, 3, 5–6, 11, 45, 99, 107–10, 112, 121, 125–7, 132, 133, 136, 139
Tocqueville Between Two Worlds (Wolin), 123, 149n2 (chap. 6)
totalitarianism, 128
Toward a Rational Society (Habermas), 131
town council, 99
"transgression with others," 101, 103, 111–19, 124–6, 129–32, 140
  civil society and, 107–11
  constitutionalism and, 132–9
  defined, 104–6
  Habermas and, 131–2
  private versus public and, 121, 136–7
  "the political" and, 123
transitional experience, 32–5, 42–3, 51, 70, 75
truth, freedom to state, 100
tuche, 72, 76, 147n2
"Two Concepts of Liberty" (Berlin), 15–16
Tyler, Tom, 107–8, 110, 111
tyranny of the majority, 11

unemployment, 84
United Kingdom, 132
"unselfing," 90, 94, 148n2
U.S. Congress, 111
U.S. Constitution, 135
U.S. Supreme Court, 133
utopia, 69–72, 77

values, 97
  equality of, 3–4
  fate and might and, 139
  Murdoch and, 89–90
  veil of ignorance, 110

"Wall Street" (movie), 84
war of all against all, 65–6
Washington Post, 1
Weber, Max, 33, 137
Weil, Simone, 42–3, 52, 57, 86, 91–2, 106
What's Fair? (Hochschild), 24
"What's Wrong with Negative Liberty" (Taylor), 27
whistleblowers, 135, 147n4 (chap. 4)
wide-awake, seeing clearly versus, 98–9
will, 35, 39, 49, 93, 130
  wounded, 78
Wille (freedom in long run), 20, 74
Willkür (arbitrary will), 20, 74
will-to-power, 44–5
Winnicott, D.W., 32, 33, 35, 37–8, 43, 53, 70, 71, 75, 103
"win or die" attitude, 81
Wittgenstein, Ludwig, 145n3
Wolfe, Alan, 3
Wolfe, Tom, 84
Wolin, Sheldon, 9, 82, 105, 123–4, 126–7, 132, 133, 136, 149n2 (chap. 6)
Wuthnow, Robert, 116–17

young people, 4–7, 11–12, 16–17, 48, 51–2, 138–9

CPSIA information can be obtained at www.ICGtesting.com
Printed in the USA
LVOW122026110112

263403LV00002B/1/A